Complete English for Cambridge Secondary 1

8

Series editor: Dean Roberts
Annabel Charles
Alan Jenkins
Tony Parkinson

WORKBOOK

Oxford excellence for Cambridge Secondary 1

OXFORD

Great Clarendon Street, Oxford, OX2 6DP, United Kingdom

Oxford University Press is a department of the University of Oxford.
It furthers the University's objective of excellence in research, scholarship, and education by publishing worldwide. Oxford is a registered trade mark of Oxford University Press in the UK and in certain other countries

© Oxford University Press 2016

The moral rights of the authors have been asserted

First published in 2016

All rights reserved. No part of this publication may be reproduced, stored in a retrieval system, or transmitted, in any form or by any means, without the prior permission in writing of Oxford University Press, or as expressly permitted by law, by licence or under terms agreed with the appropriate reprographics rights organization. Enquiries concerning reproduction outside the scope of the above should be sent to the Rights Department, Oxford University Press, at the address above.

You must not circulate this work in any other form and you must impose this same condition on any acquirer

British Library Cataloguing in Publication Data
Data available

978-0-19-836469-6

12

Paper used in the production of this book is a natural, recyclable product made from wood grown in sustainable forests. The manufacturing process conforms to the environmental regulations of the country of origin.

Printed in China by Golden Cup

Acknowledgements
The publishers would like to thank the following for permissions to use their photographs:

Cover image: David Newton/Bridgeman Art.

Artwork by Six Red Marbles.

The author and publisher are grateful for permission to reprint extracts from the following copyright material:

Malorie Blackman: *Thief* (Corgi, Doubleday Children's Books, 1995), reproduced by permission of The Random House Group Ltd.

Debjani Chatterjee: 'Hungry Ghost', copyright © Debjani Chatterjee 1997, from *A Little Bridge*, Debjani Chatterjee, Simon Fletcher and Basir Sultan Kazmi (Pennine Pens, Hebden Bridge, 1997), reproduced by permission of the author.

Berlie Doherty: *Street Child* (HarperCollins, 2009), copyright © Berlie Doherty 1993, reproduced by permission of David Higham Associates.

Carl Sandburg: lines from 'Jazz Fantasia', from *The Complete Poems of Carl Sandburg* (revised and expanded edition, Houghton Mifflin Harcourt, 2003), copyright © 1969, 1970 by Lilian Steichen Sandburg, reproduced by permission of Houghton Mifflin Harcourt Publishing Company. All rights reserved.

Any third party use of this material, outside of this publication, is prohibited. Interested parties should apply to the copyright holders indicated in each case.

Although we have made every effort to trace and contact all copyright holders before publication this has not been possible in all cases. If notified, the publisher will rectify any errors or omissions at the earliest opportunity.

Links to third party websites are provided by Oxford in good faith and for information only. Oxford disclaims any responsibility for the materials contained in any third party website referenced in this work.

®IGCSE is the registered trademark of Cambridge International Examinations.

All sample questions and answers within this publication have been written by the authors. In examination, the way marks are awarded may be different.

Table of contents

1. Foodies' delight 2
2. Amazing arts 10
3. Terrific technology 18
4. Unnatural nature 26
5. Fabulous hobbies 34
6. Alarming journeys 42
7. Heroic history 50
8. Exciting escapades 58
9. Tremendous television 66

Glossary of literary and language terms 74

Word cloud dictionary 78

Foodies' delight

My life on a plate – Food interviews

If possible, interview a family member, neighbour, or teacher about their food history. Find out about: their favourite foods as a child; what they associate with different foods, e.g. people, places, times of the year; whether food – or their tastes – have changed since they were young; what they like to eat now, and any other questions you can think of.

Alternatively, imagine that you are a journalist and decide what interesting questions you would ask a person of your age about the foods they like and why, and whether their favourite foods have always been the same. Record what your own answers would be to these questions.

My dads favourite childhood food is fishfingers. He used to associate with beans on toasts with his nan at her house because that meal he always had with her. His taste buds have changed a lot especially with the foods olives, curry, cheese and pickles. In the present he loves to eat peas, brussel sprouts and blueberries.

 **Word families**

Remember

Word families can involve all the words that come from the same root word. They can also be words that are the same word class, or words that have the same meaning (synonyms).

1. Write down all the words you can think of that include the root word 'happy'.

   Joyful, excited, wonderful, pleased, overjoyed, thankful.

2. Write down as many words as you can from the same word class as happy. (Clue: is 'happy' a noun, verb, adverb, or something else?)

   Happyness, happiest, happier ← *Switch them round*

3. Write synonyms for the word 'happy'.

   Lucky, fortunate, grateful, delighted, blessed and praised.

Foodies' delight

The expanding and shrinking sentence!

1. Rewrite each of the sentences below, adding extra detail, for example by using adjectives, adverbs, or parenthetical phrases.

   > **Remember**
   > A parenthetical phrase is a phrase that has been added into a sentence that is already complete, to provide additional information.

   a The man walked down the street.

   The man who was hungry for food down the street.

   b The door opened slowly.

   The door with the creaky hinges opened slowly.

   c The parrot flew away.

   The parrot that had been trapped flew away.

2. Rewrite each of the sentences below, to make two or more shorter, clearer sentences.

   a The children who were being chased along the beach by their friend ran very fast till they could run no more and then they decided that they would go into the woods so they ran very fast there and then they hid in there and waited until it got dark.

   The children were running away from the chaser. They decided to run in the woods until sundown.

   b Put the butter and sugar into a bowl and stir well until it's fully mixed and really smooth and then add the eggs a bit at a time and beat well until it's really smooth and then stir in the flour until it is all mixed together really well.

   Put butter and sugar into a bowl and stir it. Then add eggs a bit at a time and beat well and then stir the flour.

Lexical fields

1. Look at the following advertisement for a new breakfast cereal called Raspberry Whiz Crunch. Underline the words used to make this new cereal sound appealing to the reader.

> Are you bored with breakfast? Are you looking for something new to tingle your taste buds? Well, look no further – Raspberry Whiz Crunch is here! It's a brand new cereal made from delicious toasted wholewheat grain, crunchy clusters of oats and luscious raspberry yoghurt flavoured nuggets. Made from pure organic grain, with real juicy raspberries, this cereal tastes good and does you good too! Look out for this scrumptious new way to start your day – on supermarket shelves now!

> **Remember**
> When a writer uses a group of words to create a particular effect, it is called a lexical field.

2. Write as many words as you can to create a suitable lexical field for each of the following situations.

    a An advertisement for a car aimed at older people

    Do you wanna see up high and be comfy and spacious?, well the range rover is just for you. It's electric so you don't have to use so much energy.

    b A newspaper report about the sighting of a shark near a beach

    Few days ago a woman spotted a shark maybe in the water at the beach. Special animal diver team are getting ready to head in and close this case......

    c A school report for a student who is doing very well

    Sophie is doing very well, she can be loud in maths but she's good at art. We are pushing her and motivating so she's doing good.

Foodies' delight

Spelling bee

1. Read the text below and select the correct spelling for each gap.

   a On the way home from school, the girls had a big arguement/argumment/argument.

   b The experiment basically/basicily/basiccally involves heating the liquid up to see whether it evaporates.

   c At the beginning/begining/begginning/beginning of the film, the boy runs off into the forest.

   d The boys got completely/completly/compleetly drenched in the rain.

   e They were very disappointed/dissappointed/disapointed when their football team lost.

   f It was the most embarassing/embarrassing/embarrasing day of my entire life!

   g The environnment/enviroment/environment is one of the most important topics we study.

   h Place the hoops and balls in seperate/separate/separete crates in the gym

2. Identify **five** new spellings you need to learn and write down a way of helping you to remember each one, for example, a mnemonic, a picture, or a pattern.

   a ....
   ....

   b ....
   ....

   c ....
   ....

   d ....
   ....

   e ....
   ....

Punctuation of sentences

Read the text below.

1. Using a pencil, mark the beginning and the end of each sentence.
2. In pen, insert capital letters and end-of-sentence punctuation.

Cooking for kids and teens

1 cooking for Kids and Teens was started in 2013 by two mums who wanted their kids to learn how to cook and knew they couldn't do it alone it started with two mums and three kids in Laila's kitchen now Cooking for Kids and Teens runs classes across the country click here to find a class near you we want kids and young people
5 to learn how to make simple, wholesome food and understand that FOOD IS FUN our classes for juniors aged 6 to 11 include after school clubs, weekend workshops, preschool 'fun with food' sessions and the very popular day camps for primary kids cooking with new ingredients and flavours will encourage your child to try new foods and expand their diet they will go from cooking simple individual dishes to making
10 a whole meal from scratch we have created special sessions for teens and young adults aged 12 to 16 where they can have fun with friends and learn how to cook well for themselves when they go off to college our classes include guidance on nutrition and hygiene as well as the opportunity to invite friends and family to sample their cooking and admire their skills

Foodies' delight

Keeping in touch with friends and family

Remember

For an informal letter, you need to put your own address, but NOT the address of the person you are writing to. You need to include the date.

1. Write a short email to a friend to invite him or her to have dinner with your family for a special occasion.

~~Dear~~ 18/1/23

To Lyla!

I am inviting you to a family dinner. We have a whole roast meal and plenty to share.

2. Write a thank you letter to a relative who has given you a very unusual present, which you are not sure you like. Remember your letter should be polite and should show your appreciation.

Dear Grandma!

Thank you for my present um it was kind of you!

I have never seen anything like.

I can i say its ~~unique~~ unique.

Thank you again.

From
Yasmin.

Foodies' delight quiz

1. Write down three synonyms for the word 'scared'.
   worried, frightened, nervous.

2. **a** Write a sentence with a co-ordinating conjunction.

   b Write a sentence using a subordinating conjunction.
   I played ~~onto~~ in the garde because I wanted to.

3. Expand the following sentence in three different ways:
   The mouse ran into a hole.

   a The gray mouse ran into the big hole.

   b The scared mouse ran quickly in the hole.

   c The mouse slowly ran into the deep hole.

4. State three techniques writers use to keep the reader interested. For each technique, write an example.
   Then she went in... / Suspense.

   They had to find the magic key. / Mystery.

   Then she took her last breath! / Sad/dramatic.

5. How should you start and end:

   a a personal email or letter to your uncle?
   Dear Uncle / From Yasmin

   b a formal letter to your local politician?
   To Mr Steve / Yours sincerly.

Amazing arts

William Shakespeare and Charles Dickens are two of literature's greatest writers, but how much do you know about them?

1. Match the statements to the correct author, by drawing lines to link them to the correct writer's image. There are seven for each one. You may need to do some research.

William Shakespeare

Born in Stratford-Upon-Avon in 1564
Born in Portsmouth in 1812
A playwright and poet
Wrote 'Great Expectations'
Had a lifelong fear of being poor
Died in 1616
A novelist
Part-owned The Globe Theatre
Not much is known about his personal life
Died in 1870
Wrote 37 plays
Lived in the Victorian era
Married Anne Hathaway
Many of his novels are about social inequality

Charles Dickens

2. How many plays by William Shakespeare and novels by Charles Dickens can you name? Write them below.

<u>Plays by William Shakespeare</u>

....
....
....
....
....

<u>Novels by Charles Dickens</u>

....
....
....
....
....

Bias – being assertive

Bias is when a particular subject is preferred over an alternative. It is often used in writing to express a specific point of view and influence the reader to agree.

Being *assertive* in this context is when you write with a confidence that leads the reader to think what you say is true.

> I can't stand 'Romeo and Juliet'. All that fighting over a pointless argument leaves me with little sympathy for either side. Moreover, the ending must be the most frustrating ever in a play. I really cannot see the appeal of such a grim story.

In this extract the bias is created by:

- the dismissive tone – 'can't stand' and 'all that fighting'
- the negative assertions – '*pointless* argument'; '*little* sympathy'; '*most frustrating* ever'; '*grim* story'.

1. By changing some key words, the bias can be positive. Rewrite the extract in favour of the play.

....
....
....

2. Here are some assertions that create bias. Place each in the most appropriate box:

dull and boring   fascinating and complex   rarely encountered worse   a 'must see' event
completely absorbing   endlessly tiresome   thought-provoking   a magical experience
completely irrelevant   a new low point   surprisingly engaging   weak and insipid

Positive bias	Negative bias

Amazing arts

Synonyms and antonyms

A word that has a *similar* meaning to another word is called a synonym.

An antonym is a word that is the *opposite* of another word:

1. Complete the grid below.

Original word	Synonym	Antonym
question	query	answer
answer	response	
strong		
enemy		
begin		
difficult		
angry		
hate		
child		
lose		

2. Change the meaning of each sentence by substituting an antonym for the underlined word.

   a I would <u>always</u> choose to watch a play by Shakespeare. ....

   b Reading a novel by Charles Dickens is really <u>boring</u>. ....

   c I <u>failed</u> my Shakespeare assignment really <u>badly</u>. ....

   d *Hamlet* remains the <u>least</u> popular Shakespeare play. ....

   e The lead actor was <u>perfect</u> for the role of Hamlet. ....

Creating a caricature

A caricature is an exaggerated version of a character.

Take Miss Havisham as an example:

- The clocks were stopped at the moment she heard she had been abandoned by her husband-to-be.
- She remains in the same half-dressed state as when she heard the news.
- She has worn the same wedding dress for decades.
- The room she sits in hasn't changed or been cleaned since that day.
- She never leaves her house.
- She hates all men.
- Her skin is as yellow as the once white dress.

> Miss Havisham

1. List the words you would use to describe Miss Havisham in the box above.
2. Dickens creates memorable characters by exaggerating their appearance and actions.

Make your own caricature of one of these:

- a grumpy old lady
- an angry young man
- a spoilt child

You can use a separate sheet of paper to write down your ideas before beginning your description below.

....
....
....
....
....

Amazing arts

Semi-colons

There are three reasons to use a semi-colon:

Reason 1: As a kind of 'super' comma to mark an important break in a sentence
Reason 2: To separate a series of connected issues
Reason 3: To separate two contrasting or balanced clauses

1. Decide which reason applies in each of these sentences by writing the number in the box.

   a 'Pip is my favourite character in *Great Expectations*; Miss Havisham is the least enjoyable.'

   b Shakespeare set these plays in Italy: *Romeo and Juliet*, which is a tragedy; *The Two Gentlemen of Verona*, a comedy; *Much Ado About Nothing*, a comedy; and *The Tempest*, which is also classed as a comedy but is sometimes referred to as a romance.

   c 'I was told by a friend I wouldn't like *Hamlet*; I won't listen to him again!'

   d 'These are my favourite quotations from Shakespeare's work: 'To be or not to be' from *Hamlet*; 'All the world's a stage and we are merely players' from *As You Like It*; 'Now is the winter of our discontent' from *Richard III*; and 'What's in a name? That which we call a rose by any other name would smell as sweet' from *Romeo and Juliet*.'

2. Now it is your turn to write three sentences, each showing a different use of semi-colons.

   Sentence 1: ....

   ....

   Sentence 2: ....

   ....

   Sentence 3: ....

   ....

Creating atmosphere in your writing

Read this short extract from another Dickens novel.

> Fog everywhere. Fog up the river, where it flows among green aits and meadows; fog down the river, where it rolls defiled among the tiers of shipping and the waterside pollutions of a great (and dirty) city. Fog on the Essex marshes, fog on the Kentish heights (...) Fog in the eyes and throats of ancient Greenwich pensioners, wheezing by the firesides of their wards; fog in the stem and bowl of the afternoon pipe of the wrathful skipper, down in his close cabin; fog cruelly pinching the toes and fingers of his shivering little 'prentice boy on deck. Chance people on the bridges peeping over the parapets into a nether sky of fog, with fog all round them, as if they were up in a balloon and hanging in the misty clouds.
>
> From *Bleak House* by Charles Dickens

It is not necessary to understand every reference in the extract to work out the atmosphere Dickens has created.

1. How many times is the word 'fog' used in the extract?

   ....

2. Think of how fog seems to drift into every place possible. List three people and three locations the fog encounters.

   ....

   ....

3. **a** Choose one of the following kinds of day:
      Rainy   Windy   Snowy   Sunny

   b Write how you feel about your chosen day.

   ....

   ....

   c Write the first two sentences of your description, concentrating on creating a suitable atmosphere.

   ....

   ....

   ....

Amazing arts

Writing a script – adapting a story

Drama scripts are set out differently to works of prose:

- Each character speaks in turn in a dialogue.
- There is no narrative description.
- There is no need to use speech marks.
- Stage directions guide the actors' performance.

[Pip is standing before Miss Havisham in her living room]

"Who is it?" said the lady at the table.

"Pip, ma'am."

"Pip?"

"Mr. Pumblechook's boy, ma'am. Come—to play."

"Come nearer; let me look at you. Come close."

It was when I stood before her, avoiding her eyes, that I took note of the surrounding objects in detail, and saw that her watch had stopped at twenty minutes to nine, and that a clock in the room had stopped at twenty minutes to nine.

"Look at me," said Miss Havisham. "You are not afraid of a woman who has never seen the sun since you were born?"

I regret to state that I was not afraid of telling the enormous lie comprehended in the answer "No."

"Do you know what I touch here?" she said, laying her hands, one upon the other, on her left side.

"Yes, ma'am." (It made me think of the young man.)

"What do I touch?"

"Your heart."

"Broken!"

From *Great Expectations*, by Charles Dickens

Adapt the above extract into a drama script. The opening two lines have been completed for you.

Miss Havisham: (*sitting at the table*) Who is it?

Pip: (*standing nervously*) Pip, ma'am.

Amazing arts quiz

1. 'Born in 1564, died in 1616 and the writer of 37 plays'. Who is this describing?

   ....

2. 'Never before have I read such an amazing novel. It will keep you entertained for hours.'
   Why is this writing biased?

   ....

   ....

3. What is the main difference between a synonym and an antonym?

   ....

   ....

4. Why is Miss Havisham a caricature?

   ....

5. When might you use a semi-colon?

   ....

   ....

6. What technique does Dickens use to create the atmosphere in the following extract?

   Fog creeping into the cabooses of collier-brigs; fog lying out on the yards and hovering in the rigging of great ships; fog drooping on the gunwales of barges and small boats.

   From *Bleak House*, by Charles Dickens

   ....

   ....

7. Which four verbs help to create the atmosphere in the extract from *Bleak House*?

   ....

8. What are four key features of a drama script?

   ....

   ....

Terrific technology

Technology for us all

Technology has advanced rapidly over the last half century.

> The humble household electric vacuum cleaner is credited as one of the great inventions of the twentieth century, but did you know that the idea of using a vacuum goes back to the mid-1600s? Of course, the modern contemporary machine is a world away from its distant cousin. You can now buy a robot vacuum cleaner that works independently and uses sensors to avoid crashing into the furniture. It must work, as thousands have been sold since it went into production in 2002. If you look online, there are all kinds of vacuums for different flooring, depending on whether you have pets or not and how big your house is.

Choose any piece of technology you have at home.

1. In less than 100 words, describe your chosen piece of technology, explaining its functions and its purpose.

   ....
   ....
   ....
   ....

2. Research how your piece of technology has changed in the last few decades. Bullet point the five main differences.

   - ....
   - ....
   - ....
   - ....
   - ....

3. Are the above changes all advantages?

   ....
   ....
   ....

Regular and irregular verbs

Regular verbs are those that follow conventional rules when conjugated (e.g. changed to another tense). Irregular verbs break the rules.

'I'm a regular goody two-shoes.' 'I'm an irregular rebel.'

Present tense	Past tense	Future tense	Regular/Irregular
open	opened	open	regular
understand	**understood**	understand	irregular

1. Complete the table below.

Present tense	Past tense	Future tense	Regular/Irregular
take	**took**	will take	irregular
swarm			regular
copy	copied		
		will drink	
	wrote		
bring			
teach			
study			
stare			
complete			
	broke		

Terrific technology

Questions and answers

There are lots of different kinds of questions:

> **Open questions** – *'How are you?'*
> **Closed questions** – *'How old are you?'*
> **Leading questions** – *'Why is that television show so bad?'*
> **Rhetorical questions** – *'You don't want that, do you?'*

There are also different kinds of answers. Here are six.

Partial answer	Direct response
No response	Misdirection
Avoidance	A lie

1. Several people were asked the question: 'Would you trust a robot in your home?' Here are the responses. Decide what kind they are. The first one is done for you.

    a 'No, I wouldn't!' — <u>Direct response</u>

    b The homeowner stated, 'I don't have a home.'

    c 'Er, could you repeat the question?'

    d 'I refuse to answer that question.'

    e 'Don't you think they're really ugly?'

    f 'Maybe, it depends.'

    g 'I think homes are so expensive.'

2. In most stories, robots are programmed to tell the truth because it is more logical to do so. If this is true, which of the six kinds of responses is a robot capable of giving?

3. Identify the following types of question.

    a Can you repair that robot?

    b Isn't it wonderful that we have a robot to clean the kitchen?

    c If you didn't have a robot, you wouldn't have so much free time, would you?

    d What would happen if robots became more intelligent than people?

Using subject-specific words

Always try to use technical vocabulary linked to the subject you are writing about in order to:
- show your specific knowledge of the subject
- inform and instruct the reader
- be accurate.

Read this extract:

> Roboticists within the robotics field of science have disagreed over the moral question of artificial intelligence for decades. Some have argued the neural pathways in the positronic brain make robots much more dependable because they aren't capable of lying. Others have countered that, by using 264-bit binary code programming, the neurons in the artificial neural network can be taught to make the robot autonomous.

1. There are ten subject-specific technical terms in the passage. Can you find them?

   ....
   ....
   ....
   ....
   ....

2. Which technical term appears twice?

   ....

3. Why do you think it appears twice?

   ....
   ....

4. Now it is your turn to create a technical vocabulary. Choose an area of science or technology you know, such as physics, chemistry, biology, computing.

   Write at least ten technical terms in the space below. If you can find twenty, you're an expert!

Terrific technology

Fitting sentences to purpose

You can control pace, tone, atmosphere and how much you want the reader to know through your sentence construction.

1. Read the text below and write a sentence better suited to that purpose.

   Excuse me, please, but I am in need of assistance. I appear to be in danger of being eaten by this very large shark swimming at a fast pace towards my current position. I believe scientists call it 'Carcharodon Carcharias' but you would know it as a 'Great White'. I can tell this by the size of its mouth and the number of teeth closing in on me.

   ....

2. Aanjay is trying to write a scientific report on an incident in a laboratory but it needs a lot more information.

   Have fun helping him by adding more information to each box.

   'It was yesterday.'

   'I was doing an experiment.'

   'It went wrong.'

   'I'm okay but the lab isn't.'

Words with similar meanings

Each word in the English language has its own individual definition but often there are words with a *similar* meaning that can be grouped together.

These are called synonyms.

Take the word *aeroplane* as an example:

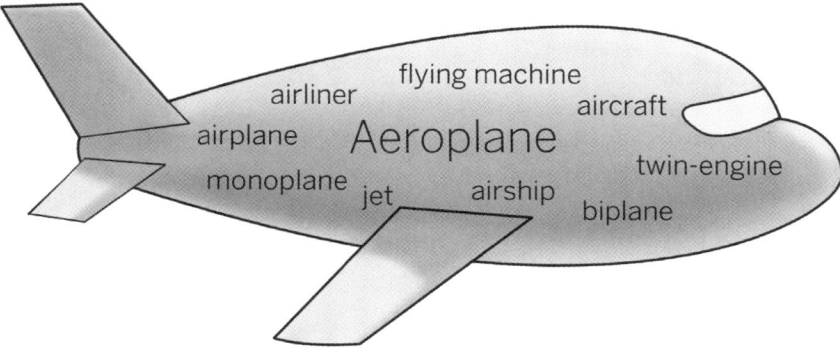

1. Add at least five synonyms to each box, but aim for ten each.

Motor car	Building

2. Underline the words which do not belong in this group.

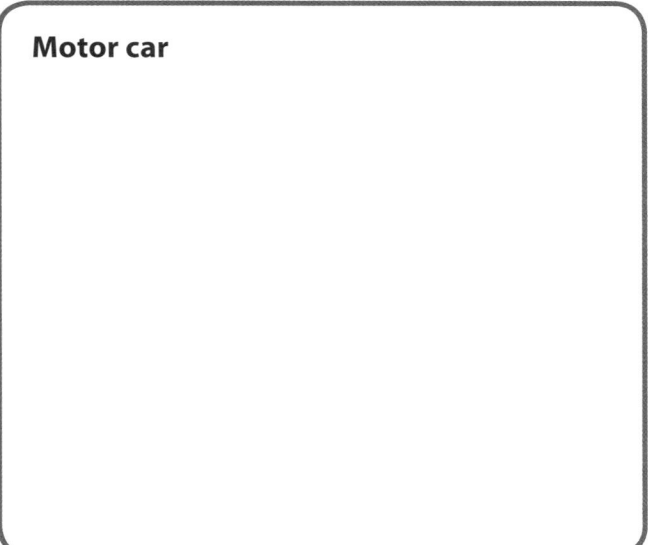

star   galaxy   Milky Way   orbit   moon   submarine   sun
weather   asteroids   atmosphere   aeroplane   comet   meteor
cosmic   constellation   horoscope   ocean

The group theme is ....

Terrific technology

Writing a speech – the opening

This is an effective opening from a speech made by a salesman selling robots:

> 'How many times have you wished for a magic wand to do all your jobs around the house? Why is it you have to look after your baby sister at exactly the time your friends call? Who hasn't wished they had more 'me' time? If these scenarios apply to you then I have the perfect solution. Meet Robot 101 – your new best friend.'

It begins by asking questions to engage the audience before introducing the product as the answer to all your problems.

1. Here are some beginnings. For each one say whether you think it is effective or not and why.

    a 'I haven't really prepared anything but I suppose I could talk for a few minutes about robots.'

    ....

    ....

    b 'Friends, colleagues, valued customers past and future, I am here to offer you an unbelievable opportunity.'

    ....

    ....

    c 'I am Robot 101, your new best friend. You can call me Rob. We are going to have such fun together when you own me. I can perform many functions and I will never leave you. My purpose is to make your life wonderful.'

    ....

    ....

2. You are the salesman now; write the opening paragraph of your speech.

    ....

    ....

    ....

    ....

    ....

Terrific technology quiz

1. 'Why would you ever want to own a robot?'
   What kind of question is this? Does it need an answer?

   ....

2. What is the difference between a regular and irregular verb?

   ....

   ....

3. 'Do you agree that GM crops are dangerous?' Answer this question using:
   a A direct response: ....
   b A misdirection: ....

4. Add three more examples to expand this grouping of subject-specific terms related to growing crops: *tillage; crop rotation; planting; ploughing; irrigating; fertilising.*

   ....

5. Which sentence is more suitable for its purpose? Why?
   a 'It may be a good time to tell everyone that I have made a rather large mistake when mixing the chemicals for my experiment and it seems there has been a somewhat violent reaction which could cause a major incident that threatens both us and the laboratory'.
   b 'Run, the lab's going to explode!'

   ....

6. Connect these synonyms to make matching pairs.

robot	satellite
moon	missile
planet	meteor
falling star	world
rocket	android

7. Why is this effective as an opening to a speech?

   'Isn't it remarkable that we still don't know enough about GM crops? With all this scientific knowledge, we are still no nearer to knowing if they will cause long-term harm. Doesn't this make you feel somewhat uneasy? I know I feel that way.'

   ....

   ....

Unnatural nature

Speaking and listening

Debating

Here's your chance to have another go at debating. You'll need at least one other person to prepare a speech opposing what you say.

You can choose your own motion, but here are some ideas to help you.

- Homework is of no use to anybody.
- The law should be reformed to allow people to drive at 12 years.
- There are too many rules and regulations in our country.

Now prepare some brief notes to remind you what you will say. Think of at least three arguments and work out how you would explain each one of them.

Argument 1 ....

....

....

Explanation ....

....

....

Argument 2 ....

....

....

Explanation ....

....

....

Argument 3 ....

....

....

Explanation ....

....

....

Argument 4 ....

....

....

Explanation ....

....

....

How I will end my speech: ....

....

....

Writing a letter

Mary Kingsley was a remarkable woman. She died over a hundred years ago, but if she were alive today she would be greatly admired.

Here is another very brief extract from Mary's journal.

> It was a wonderfully lovely quiet night with no light save that from the stars. (...) I paddled leisurely across the lake to the shore on the right, and seeing crawling on the ground some large glow-worms, drove the canoe on to the bank among some hippo grass, and got out to get them. (...) I felt the earth quiver under my feet, and heard a soft big soughing sound, and looking round saw I had dropped in on a hippo banquet. I made out five of the immense brutes round me, so I softly returned to the canoe and shoved off (...)

Imagine Mary Kingsley is still alive. **Write her a letter inviting her to come to talk to the students in your school. You should aim to write three paragraphs. State your reason for writing, why you think the students would enjoy hearing her speak, and give a brief plan for her visit.**

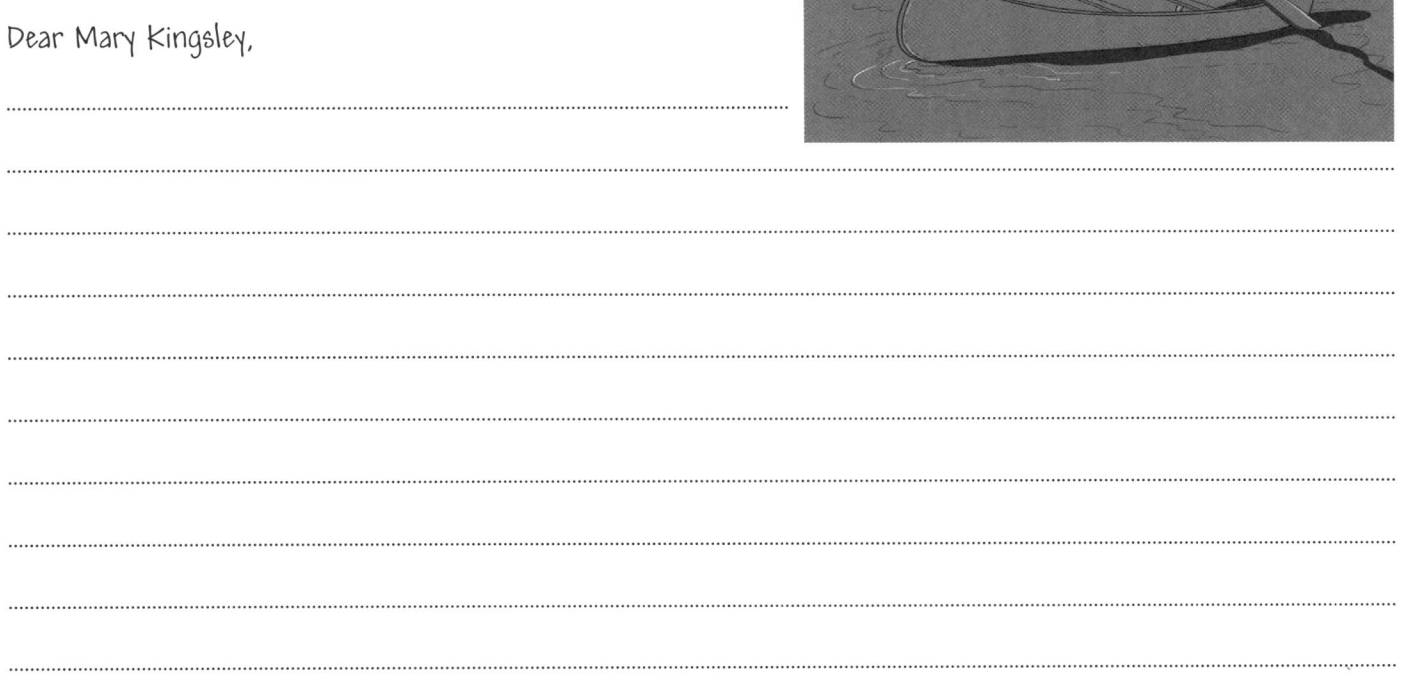

Dear Mary Kingsley,

....

....

....

....

....

....

....

....

....

....

Yours sincerely,

Unnatural nature

Know which tense to use!

Using the simple present tense, continue this advice from a teacher.

"Claudia, I try my best to teach you English, but every day you come into the classroom and just don't concentrate. When I ask you to get your book out you ....

....

....

....,"

Now use the simple past as if you were observing the lesson.

Claudia listened quietly to her teacher and then nodded her head and smiled a little smile. ....

....

....

....

Pretend you are Claudia and you have just got home from school. Finish this entry in your diary, using the present continuous tense.

I am sitting by my window, drinking a glass of lovely pineapple juice. The birds in the garden are singing sweetly ....

....

....

....

Now pretend to be Claudia's parent telling the teacher the following day how Claudia had explained her lack of attention in the lesson. Use the past continuous tense.

"Claudia told us last night that she was struggling to focus because ....

....

....

....,"

Reading about settings

Read these tips for visitors to the Arctic and answer the questions.

"Don't get me wrong, because the tundra is not the most dangerous holiday destination, but there are three things you should look out for. The first is a whiteout. You can be walking down the street when out of nowhere a snowstorm envelopes you. Everything turns white and you can only see a few centimetres in front of you. You are instantly disoriented and the temperature plummets to -50 degrees Celsius. And that's only in town. Another problem is the polar bear. No, he is not friendly at all, and attacks by polar bears are usually fatal – for humans. People who live near the bears usually go about in groups and always, repeat always, carry rifles. Good luck! Finally, if you want a comfortable night's rest, beware of mosquitoes and black flies. If you go where the mosquitoes hang out, you need long-sleeved shirts and tough trousers, and you should make sure you have a good-quality insect repellent. Otherwise, welcome to the tundra!"

1. List three things people should be careful of when they go to the tundra.

   ....

2. What do you think a whiteout is?

   ....

3. Which word indicates that it suddenly gets very cold? Check the spelling.

   ....

4. Which word indicates that you have no idea where you are? Check the spelling.

   ....

5. Why does the speaker say "good-quality" when he describes insect repellent?

   ....

6. Why might you be convinced that polar bears are seriously dangerous?

   ....

7. Why or why not would you enjoy visiting the tundra?

   ....
   ....

Unnatural nature

Using conditional sentences

Here are some ideas for you to think about.

- If animals could speak ....
- If dinosaurs ruled the world ....
- If children were in charge of everything ....
- If I can ...., you can.
- If it doesn't stop raining ....

Write your ideas below.

If only...

- If only I were two metres tall ....
  ....

- If only you were a millionaire ....
  ....

- If only we had not got locked in at school ....
  ....

- .... there'd be enough food for everyone in the world and no more starvation.

- .... there'd be no more war.

What if...

- What if we all decided to turn up to school ten minutes late?
  ....
  ....

- What if I had been more helpful when my aunt was so busy?
  ....
  ....

Now practise making your own sentences using *if*.

....
....
....

Image explorer

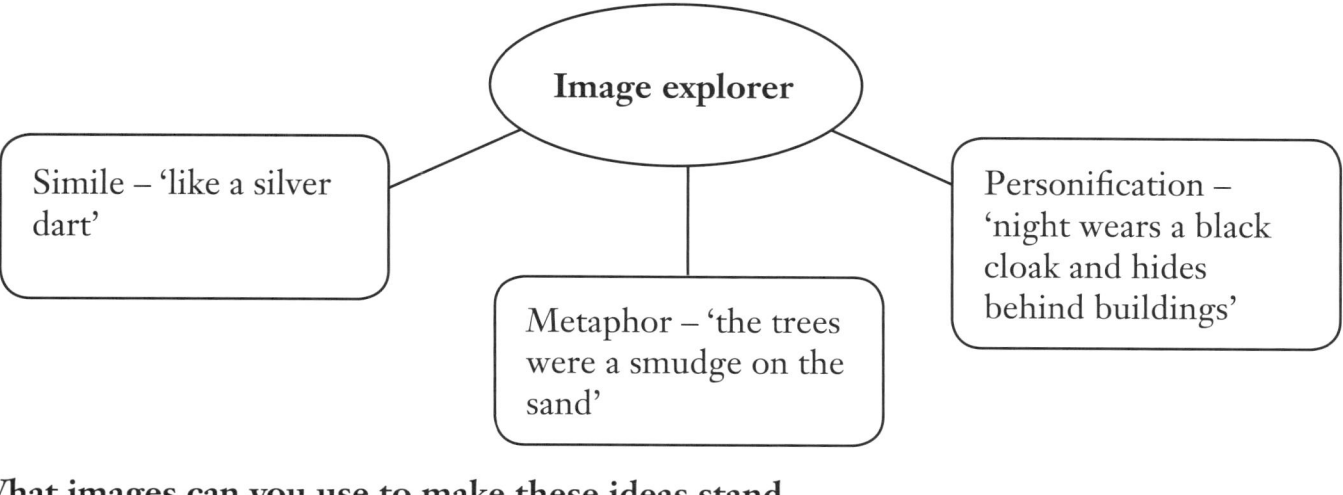

What images can you use to make these ideas stand out more clearly? Try to use a simile, a metaphor and personification for each scene.

The sounds in a busy market ....

....

A fast-growing creeper in the jungle ....

....

Picking up something unpleasant by mistake ....

....

The Arctic Circle ....

....

Someone's room after a burglar has broken in ....

....

A scene of your own connected with nature ....

....

Unnatural nature

Writing a summary

"Mum, there was this man told us all about kangaroos and their babies – Joeys they're called. I didn't know you could eat kangaroos – I think it's cruel, but the man says there's very little fat. Mind you, there are 34 million of them in Australia – that's where they live. Joeys live in a pouch on their mum's front. Did you know they can leap along at 20 to 25 kilometres per hour? He said they are shy animals and they are nocturnal and come out at night. They come from a family that means big foot. I suppose that's why they can leap along so fast. And they can swim!"

The student did well to remember all this information, but there's no order to it. **Can you get 11 facts into some sort of order to write a clear summary?**

There are 108 words. Aim to write 60– 65 words for your summary.

Notes

Fact 1: ....

Fact 2: ....

Fact 3: ....

Fact 4: ....

Fact 5: ....

Fact 6: ....

Fact 7: ....

Fact 8: ....

Fact 9: ....

Fact 10: ....

Fact 11: ....

My summary: ....

....

....

....

Word count: ....

Unnatural nature quiz

Here's a quick quiz to see how much you remember about what you learnt in this unit.

1. What are two good topics for a debate?

   a ....

   b ....

2. What tense is this sentence using?

   I am sitting here watching the elephants soaking themselves with water.

   a past continuous   b simple present

   c present continuous   d simple past.

3. Write a sentence about dolphins using the past continuous tense.

   ....

4. In 30 seconds, write down 10 words associated with cold.

   a ....   b ....
   c ....   d ....
   e ....   f ....
   g ....   h ....
   i ....   j ....

5. What two words in this list mean roughly the same thing: *hollow, oval-shaped, crescent, elliptical, circular*? Underline them.

6. Which of these *if* sentences is definite, which is likely, and which is improbable? Write 'D', 'L' or 'I' next to each.

   a If we get too close to that whale, it will scare us. ....

   b If that whale splashes us, we will get wet. ....

   c If I'd known we were going to see a whale, I'd have died. ....

7. Put these in order of which you think best personifies the sea.

   a a monster   b an angel

   c an angry soldier   d an old man

8. List three things you must **not** do when writing a summary.

   ....

   ....

Fabulous hobbies

Market research

If you were to write your own magazine, you would need to do some research and planning.

Like any writer, you need to make your product appealing to your target audience.

Research

1. Look at two magazines aimed at a teenage audience.
2. Fill out this table based on your findings by ticking to show which features each magazine has.

	Features found in first magazine title	Features found in second magazine title
Engaging front cover		
Bold, easy to spot title		
Index of features		
A mixture of fonts		
Colour images		
Editorials		
Reviews		
Reports		
Interviews		
Human interest articles		
Topical articles		
Advertisements		
Letters page		
Games page		
Horoscopes		

Planning

Based on your research, make a list of the contents you think should be included in your school 'sports and hobbies' magazine.

....

....

....

Editorials

Editorials are usually written by the magazine editor. They set the tone for the magazine and introduce an important theme. They are a mixture of facts and opinions.

Here is an extract from a sports magazine's editorial:

> 'The champions are crowned, those relegated lick their wounds, and thousands of devotees desperately start searching for something to do on a Saturday afternoon for the next two months. Yes, you've guessed it – another English Premier League season has reached its predictable conclusion. But, what have we learnt? Very little I would hazard to guess.
>
> The Premier League, or EPL as it is commonly known, continues to grow. Watched in over 200 countries with a potential worldwide audience of over 4 billion people, the EPL has become a juggernaut of such size and scope that it will take some stopping. Add to that a domestic television deal worth one billion pounds sterling and an internationally generated income of over two billion Euros and you begin to see the bigger picture... and the bigger problem.'

1. Pick out three facts used in the editorial.

   ....
   ....

2. What do you think is the editor's opinion of the EPL? Support your answer with evidence from the text.

   ....
   ....

3. Although the EPL is the subject of the editorial, what do you think it is really about?

   ....
   ....

4. Write the third and final paragraph of the editorial.

   ....
   ....
   ....

Fabulous hobbies

Using the prefix *in–*.

The prefix *in–* usually changes the meaning of a word to its opposite meaning. For example:

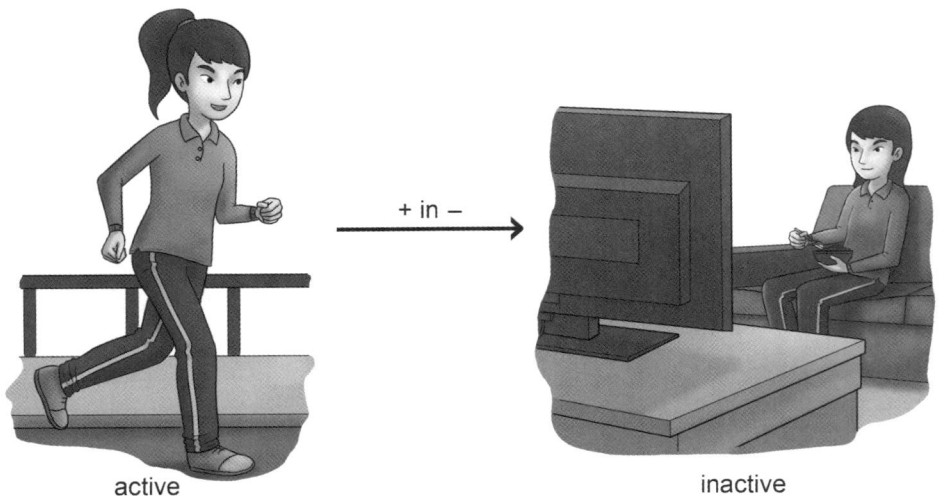

active   inactive

Look at the following words and read sentences 1–6, then choose the best word to fill in each of the gaps.

- inactivity
- insecure
- inconsiderate
- insincere
- indecision
- insufficient
- independent

1. The team lost because of too much ....

2. A round the world yachtsman needs to be ....

3. .... is a state of doing nothing that leads to a lack of fitness.

4. No one believed the tennis star as he was being ....

5. The defence conceded five goals because it was ....

6. The club could not pay the players' wages because there were .... funds.

36

Using vocabulary for effect

The effect a writer wants to create is linked to the point of view being expressed. This is the perspective and will differ depending on the bias of the writer.

Read these two perspectives on the same subject.

A 'I find stamp collecting to be a most intriguing and rewarding hobby. Each stamp has its own unique and captivating history that is both informative and entertaining in equal measures. In addition, I have met many fellow philatelists who themselves are fascinating characters with countless appealing tales to tell.'

B 'Never in all my days have I come across a more pointless, boring, and mind-numbing hobby than collecting stamps. Paying huge amounts of hard-earned money for tatty pieces of second-hand paper seems to me an exercise in futility. It is a hobby for anti-social and uninteresting people. Who in their right mind wants to learn about stamps anyway?'

1. Create your own positive and negative word clouds by choosing words and phrases from the extracts.

Positive	Negative

2. Choose a sport or hobby that you either strongly like or strongly dislike. Write a descriptive paragraph from your biased perspective.

Fabulous hobbies

Using punctuation accurately

Colons

Colons are used to introduce an example or explanation within a sentence. They are also used to introduce a list.

1. Desiree is having problems with her use of colons. Can you help her by adding the correct punctuation below?

    a 'Ever since I was a child I have listened to all kinds of music slow fast modern and old-style.'

    b 'It would be wonderful if I could meet my favourite rock star I would be overawed.'

    c To start a band you need guitars keyboards drums and a singer.

    d 'I love the sound of a steel guitar it is so relaxing.'

    e 'I've played live concerts in all the world's major cities London Cairo New York Mumbai Moscow.'

Brackets and dashes

Brackets (parentheses) and **dashes** can be used to add extra information to sentences and – in addition – dashes can create a change of emphasis.

2. Write out the sentences again, adding brackets or dashes.

    a Beyonce was born in Houston Texas but has moved to Los Angeles California having once lived in New York.

    b She is a now a solo artist having made her name in the group Destiny's Child and has sold over 75 million records worldwide.

    c Beyonce has won many music awards and is a leading figure in the music industry she is also a successful businesswoman.

When to write informally

Magazines are a mixture of formal and informal written pieces.

1. Match the type of writing to the purpose and decide whether it is formal, informal, or both.

Feature	Purpose	Formal or informal?
Editorial	Offers opinion on topic	Formal
Index of features		
Review		
Letters page		
Advertisements		
Reports		
Interviews		
Articles		

The letters page may be more informal in both style and appearance. Here is an example:

Dear Sel, I'm having real trouble convincing my dad that he should let me try trial biking. I've seen it on TV and it looks so cool. I don't care about falling off but me dad says it's a fool's sport and there's no way he wants me to end up in hospital. What can I do? All me mates are doin' it and I'm sitting at home writing letters. Please, please help me!!!

2. What features of the writing tell you this is an informal piece?

....

....

3. Write a reply to Sel in a similar informal style.

....

....

....

....

Fabulous hobbies

Writing a review

This is an extract from a review that has been written in a formal style and from a clear perspective.

> When it first appeared, the Xbox One was to many a huge disappointment. Overpriced and underpowered, it was no match for the rival PS4. Where Sony had delivered, Microsoft had failed. For all its hype and range of advanced features, the Xbox could not compete at the most basic level against the PS4 – as a games console it came second every time.
>
> Now let us move forward in time to the present. What a transformation has occurred! No longer the poor little sibling, the Xbox has found its feet and become the alpha male the company promised it would be. More powerful, less expensive, and with a quality controller, the vision has come to fruition.'

1. According to the review, what were the original problems with the Xbox One?

   ....

2. How did it compare against the PS4 as a games console?

   ....

3. Why is it now a better games console?

   ....

4. What is the perspective (angle) that the writer uses?

   ....

Now it is your turn to write a review. You can choose from a film, book, television show, computer game or console, or any subject connected to hobbies.

My review of ....

....

....

....

....

....

....

Culture unit quiz time

1. Which of these features in a magazine should be written in a more formal writing style, and which in an informal style? Place either an **F** or an **I** alongside each feature.

   Editorials ....   Interviews ....   Advertisements ....

   Reviews ....   Human interest articles ....   Letters page ....

   Reports ....   Topical articles ....   Games page ....

2. Underline the statement below that best explains why this is a typical piece of editorial writing.

   'Another English Premier League season has reached its predictable conclusion. But what have we learnt? Very little, I would hazard to guess.'

   a   It is about football and is written in a formal tone.

   b   It contains a question that is then answered.

   c   It introduces a theme and offers an opinion that sets the tone.

   d   I love football and I want to read this kind of article.

3. What do you think this idiom means?

   'It was a game of two halves.'

   ....

4. Underline the six words that create a positive perspective:

   'Walking delights me. I love to spend the day freely wandering the magnificent hills near my home. I am blessed to have such a marvellous resource so close by.'

5. Add the correct punctuation to the sentence below.

   These four clubs were founding members of the Premier League Liverpool, Manchester United Arsenal and Chelsea.

6. Which of these features is not typical of a review? Underline your answer.

   a   A clear perspective or angle   b   A judgement

   c   A question and answer section   d   Quotations

   e   Formal writing

7. Give two reasons why you would use a dash in a sentence.

   ....

   ....

Alarming journeys

Discussing journeys

Find two or three people to share a discussion. Choose one of the four journeys below and discuss in your group how you think the journey might be difficult or scary.

Before you start your discussion, you might wish to make brief notes of your ideas to share.

A climb you might go on

....

....

....

A journey involving water

....

....

....

A journey to a new city or town

....

....

....

Be prepared to give a summary of your discussion to the class.

Unpacking words

Some words are like parcels: they have different layers of meaning to be unpacked.

When you hear a word, it makes you think of other things. When you are writing, this helps you to choose the word you want, and when you are reading, it prompts your imagination.

For example, think about noises. To start you off, here's a very simple sentence:

The creature made a noise.

Read the following sentences, which use more powerful words than *noise*. Write single words or short phrases to describe what you imagine when you read them.

The creature growled. ....

It groaned. ....

There was a buzzing. ....

It whimpered. ....

At night I heard howling in the wood. ....

For an answer he just grunted. ....

Year 8, what is this cacophony? ....

Stop grumbling! ....

A twittering came from the box. ....

Cackling, she turned slowly. ....

Write a sentence or two to describe the sounds of a large, violent, and angry animal that has just become aware of your presence.

....

....

....

....

....

Alarming journeys

A prepositional verse

Sometimes you can put several prepositional phrases together, a bit like joining pieces of string – although this can get rather clumsy.

Here's a verse made almost entirely out of prepositional phrases. **Work out which preposition goes at the beginning of each line.** All the prepositions could be different.

I met a creature
.... the top step
.... the staircase
.... the carpet
.... six creepy-crawly legs
.... five centimetres long

I took it
.... its hiding place
.... my shaking hand
.... greatest peril
.... my fragile sanity

I couldn't bear to kill it so it went
.... a pretty little box
.... the windowsill
.... the floral curtains
.... some later time

My annoying little sister happened to find the box and, being inquisitive, had to discover what was in it.

Ha! Ha! Very Ha! Ha!

Try writing your own verse using a string of prepositional phrases.

....

....

....

....

....

Making a big splash!

What is the difference between an object hitting the water and making the droplets fly everywhere and a ripe peach dropped onto a concrete path?

Answer: one goes 'splash!' and the other goes 'splat!'

Think about the sound *spla*. Why does one word end in *–sh* and the other in *–t*? They're both examples of onomatopoeia.

Here's another example for you to work out.

Say *push* and *pull* several times slowly. Act the movements out by swaying your body in time to the two words. What happens in your mouth when you say these words? How are they different?

....

....

This is part of a poem about the sounds made by instruments in a jazz band. **Underline the words that you think are examples of onomatopoeia and discuss why you have chosen them.**

Jazz Fantasia

Drum on your drums, batter on your banjoes,
sob on the long cool winding saxophones.

Go to it, O jazzmen.

Sling your knuckles on the bottoms of the happy tin pans, let your trombones ooze, and go husha-husha-hush with the slippery sand-paper.

From 'Jazz Fantasia' by Carl Sandburg

Alarming journeys

Vocabulary word search

There are 10 words in this word search that come from the poem 'Drifting'.

When you have found each of the words, choose the correct word to write in the spaces below the grid. The first one has been done for you.

W	J	P	Y	W	K	X	D	E	Z	Q	Q
S	C	R	Y	S	T	A	L	E	P	O	Z
T	H	O	U	G	H	T	S	L	M	L	L
E	T	F	X	T	C	O	C	X	A	Z	A
H	F	O	Q	D	S	A	K	J	T	J	T
Z	N	U	U	F	F	A	Z	O	J	B	I
Q	B	N	Q	E	T	E	R	N	A	L	T
H	A	D	Q	S	L	E	D	G	E	S	U
C	X	A	W	N	U	D	R	I	F	T	D
W	I	R	X	S	U	R	E	L	Y	S	E
E	S	W	Q	G	N	H	R	L	V	D	D
Z	Z	S	O	L	I	T	U	D	E	C	Q

SLEDGES
LATITUDE
ETERNAL
THOUGHTS
SURELY
DRIFT
AXIS
PROFOUND
CRYSTAL
SOLITUDE

1. Which word means lasting forever, not ending or changing? Answer: ETERNAL

2. Which word is a verb meaning to move very slowly?
   ....

3. Which word is an adverb?
   ....

4. Which word describes vehicles designed to travel over snow and ice?
   ....

5. Which word describes a line through the centre of a spinning object? What is the spinning object referred to in 'Drifting'?
   ....

Creative writing

In the recording you heard about some students who had to go to school, making their way across a perilous bridge over a dangerous river. Imagine that you lived in the village that was cut off and this is the first time you have to cross the bridge with your friends. Write about the experience. How did you feel as you began the crossing, what happened, and how did you feel when you got to the other side?

Alarming journeys

Responding to a poem

Read the following poem, where the poet journeys back to the local market she visited as a child, and reflects on how much it has changed. Answer the questions that follow.

Hungry Ghost

Today I went shopping with my father
after many years. I was back
in time to when I'd follow Grandfather
to the market, smelling the spicy scents,
drinking the sights and mingling with the shouts.
Neither buyer nor seller, I would float
like a restless spirit hungry for life.

The market is bigger. I have grown too.
There are more goods as distances have shrunk.
The prices are higher. I understand
about money and, alas, its bondage
of buyers and sellers. Almost I wish
I was again that hungry ghost, watchful
and floating through the world's noisy bazaar.

'Hungry Ghost' by Debjani Chatterjee

> **Remember**
> A metaphor is used to represent someone or something as something else.

1. How does the poet describe the atmosphere at the market in the first verse? Use examples to support your answer.

   ....

   ....

2. The last line of the poem refers to the 'world's noisy bazaar'. What might this metaphor mean?

   ....

   ....

3. What is the poet's wish at the end of the poem?

   ....

   ....

Journeys unit quiz

1. Look at the words below. What do they mean and how are they different? Fill in the table.

	Definition	**Different from *journey* because…**
journey		
trip		
expedition		
tour		

2. Link the words to their definitions.

preposition	A group of words that form a unit within a sentence, often without a verb
phrase	A phrase with a preposition and its object
prepositional phrase	Used with a noun or pronoun to show how things are related, e.g., place, position, or time

3. In 'Drifting', the writer uses the word 'fly' twice. What is the difference between the two instances?

   ....

   ....

4. **a** Underline words below that create a quiet and a calm atmosphere.

   Moveless fish in the water gleam

   By silver reeds in a silver stream.

   b Explain your answer.

   ....

   ....

   ....

   ....

Heroic history

Speaking and listening – conducting interviews

Imagine you host a breakfast programme for a local radio. Every day you interview someone. You finish by asking them to choose a piece of their favourite music.

You are looking for your next guest to interview. The person could speak to you as themselves or pretend to be someone else.

Plan who you will interview. For example, you may choose:

- a friend to interview about hobbies or a recent achievement, such as in sports
- someone pretending to be a teacher or a police officer
- a musician who has just performed for the first time.

Before you start the interview, write notes on four questions you plan to ask before the person's favourite piece of music is requested. These notes will act as a reminder. If you listen carefully, you may be able to ask other questions that arise from something the person says.

Interviews on radio sound like conversations. Interviewers don't usually just say, for example, "What's your favourite hobby?" Instead an interviewer might say something like, "I've heard that you are a very keen long distance runner and that you practise several times a week. Doesn't that take a lot of your spare time?"

1. ....

2. ....

3. ....

4. ....

Remember you have an audience to entertain – so how will you introduce your interview, and how will you finish it?

The introduction: ....

The end of the interview: ....

Your opinion

When someone asks you to explain why you like one story, poem, or play more than another, you need to give reasons. It is not enough to say, "It was exciting" or, if you didn't like it, "It was boring".

You have read two very short stories, one about Catahecassa and the other about Beowulf. **Now it's your chance to write about which story you preferred, and why. If you can't decide which you think is the better of the two, explain why.**

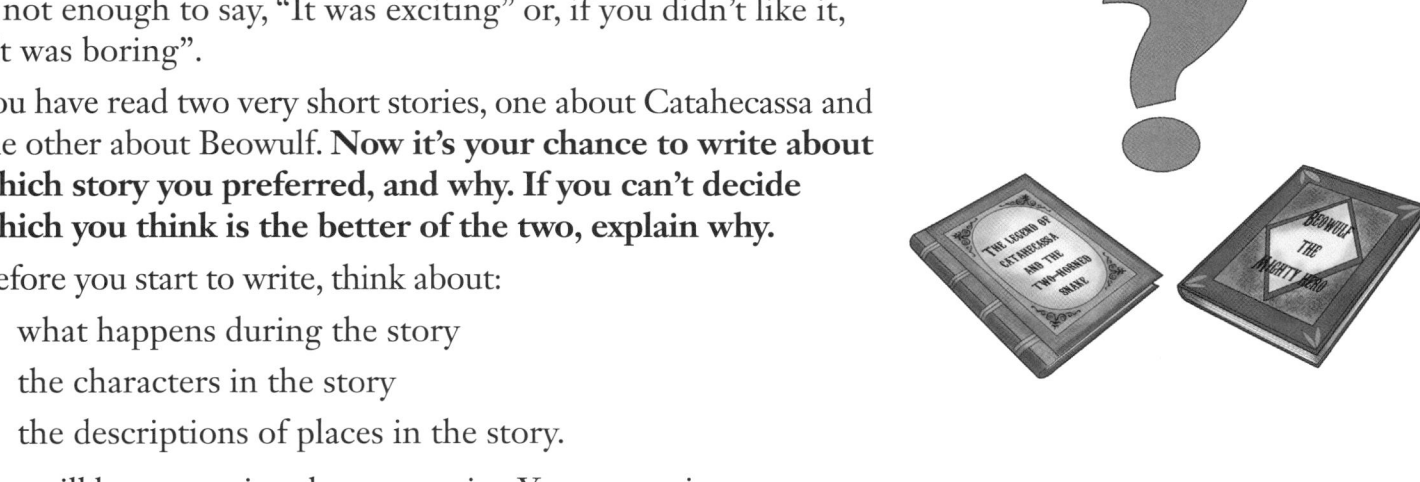

Before you start to write, think about:

- what happens during the story
- the characters in the story
- the descriptions of places in the story.

You will be comparing the two stories. You may write:

'In the story of the two-horned snake ... but in the story of Beowulf ....'

'The Legend of Catahecassa' and 'Beowulf, The Mighty Hero'

....
....
....
....
....
....
....
....
....
....
....
....
....
....
....

Heroic history

Crazy paragraphs

The eight sentences on this page make one paragraph, but they are in the wrong order.

Decide on the right order and write the paragraph below.

I had overslept so there was absolutely no time for my daily shower.

With a sinking feeling, I realised I'd be late for work.

It was already 8.40 a.m.

It was eight o'clock!

Yesterday I woke up from a long sleep and looked at my watch.

Of course it wouldn't start and therefore I'd have to catch a bus.

I threw on my clothes and rushed downstairs.

Grabbing a piece of bread, I rushed to my car.

Dragonland

Dragons exist in the myths of nations all over the world. Heroes often fought them. **Read this article about dragons.**

Have you seen pictures of dragons with their long tails, which often have sharp spikes and even an arrowhead on the end? No one knows where the idea of a dragon came from, but originally the word was Greek and it meant a big snake or a water snake.

Sometime in history, artists gave dragons legs and huge, flappy wings and they started to look more like dinosaurs. Chinese and Vietnamese dragons were friendly. In China, they were associated with power and majesty, and in Vietnam a dragon brought rain. However, in most places the dragon was a savage beast with hard skin looking like armour and it had to be overcome by a hero.

Certainly, pictures of dragons, with their forked tongues and pointed teeth, are all very similar. Some artists show them flying, but this is rare. Others show them breathing fire, although not all dragons do this. Often the back of the dragon's neck, like the rest of its body, is covered with what look like very sharp spikes. Of course dragons, which live in rivers or in underground lairs, are very large creatures.

What would you expect to see in a picture of an evil dragon? List eight features.

1. ....
2. ....
3. ....
4. ....
5. ....
6. ....
7. ....
8. ....

Now use your notes to write a paragraph about the appearance of the dragon in the picture. Write in sentences and don't copy phrases from the article.

....
....
....
....
....

Heroic history

Don't argue with me!

You can use discourse markers to change the direction of an argument. **Take part in this argument, which is set out like a play.** Here you will be using discourse markers that express contrast.

Huang: I think school uniform is a really good idea because I look really neat and tidy.

You: Well, that's true. However, ...
....
....

Huang: I can see your argument about some of the boys who make the uniform look untidy but, nevertheless, ...
....
....

Another thing is that if everyone wears the same, it stops people who are rich showing off.

You: Yes, but it also stops individuality. I respect your arguments, but in spite of what you say, ...
....

Now here is a Principal speaking at assembly. Fill in the gaps in what she has to say. The discourse markers here will show the consequences of people's actions.

Principal: Today I have good news and not so good news.
I am very happy to report that the gymnastics team have won their area tournament. As a result, ...
On a less happy note, four students in the last two days have been reported to me for not wearing their school uniform properly. Consequently, ...
....

Finally, there has been far too much noise going on in the area outside my meeting room. You probably know that I receive many visitors and we need quiet to discuss matters of importance to us all. Therefore, I have decided ....
....

Pin down the meaning!

Do the following three activities. You'll need to find someone else to take part in the first two.

1. Below are six definitions of common words. Read one definition out at a time and the other person has to guess the word. Write the words in the spaces.

    a the larva of some kinds of fly: ....

    b the molten rock that flows from a volcano: ....

    c the adjective to describe a volcano that has not erupted for a long time: ....

    d a wooden or concrete beam that the tracks of a railway rest on: ....

    e a wagon on a North American railroad: ....

    f a light cardboard or plastic container: ....

2. Act out the following and the other person has to guess what they are:

    dice   statue   oblong
    handkerchief playing any musical instrument   feeling nervous

3. Come up with a definition for each of the following words and write it in the space.

    a *errand:* ....

    b *equator:* ....

    c *escalator:* ....

    d *eruption:* ....

    e *estuary:* ....

    f *eternal*: ....

4. Compare each of your definitions in **3a–f** with one from a dictionary. Which was better?

Heroic history

Writing an alternative ending

Read your story about a superhero again, looking in particular at the last two paragraphs. There is a turning point when things probably get better for the superhero. Then there is an exciting climax and the ending follows.

Imagine things had turned out very differently. Write a new version of paragraphs 4 and 5. If it was a happy story before, make it tragic now, or the other way round. The words you choose will help to change the atmosphere of the story, perhaps from joy to sadness.

Heroic history quiz

1. The two-horned snake had magical powers of magnetism. Explain how the magnetism would show itself and why the legend said that the snake was magical.

   ....

   ....

2. Write a sentence that links these three words: *legend*, *tradition*, and *fiction*.

   ....

3. 'My little sister let out a howl like a wounded animal because I told her not to eat any more chocolate.' What term do we use for 'like a wounded animal' and what does it tell you about the girl's howl?

   ....

4. Discourse markers are:
   - [ ] words that are always adjectives
   - [ ] words and phrases that show the direction of an argument
   - [ ] arguments that are for and against an issue
   - [ ] the first sentence in a paragraph.

5. Explain what is meant by a turning point in a story.

   ....

6. Solve these anagrams for words that mean ways of talking together.

   Aunt Germ: ....

   Overcoats Inn: ....

   Eat bed: ....

7. An octogenarian is 79 years old – true or false? Give a reason for your answer.

   ....

8. The most exciting part of a story that I write should be:
   - [ ] at the beginning
   - [ ] in the last sentence
   - [ ] in the second paragraph
   - [ ] near the end of the story.

Exciting escapades

My favourite book

_____'s favourite book

Name of favourite book

....

Author(s)

....

Illustration of my favourite book

Book summary

....

....

....

....

Reasons why this is my favourite book

Identify techniques used by the author where possible.

....

....

....

....

Favourite character (with explanation)

....

....

....

Remember

Writers can start books and stories by:
- describing the setting
- introducing the character
- addressing the reader
- going straight into the action
- providing history/background to the story
- including speech/conversation
- reflecting on what has happened
- suggesting what the story is going to be about
- withholding information from the reader.

1. Look at some of your favourite books and stories, and find three opening sentences that you think are really good.

   Copy them out and explain the technique used by the writer.

   Has the technique been used successfully?

   i ....

   ii ....

   iii ....

2. Now write an opening sentence for three different stories. Each one should really 'hook' the reader. Try to include a hint as to the kind of story it's going to be.

   i ....

   ii ....

   iii ....

Using adverbs and adverbials

1. Complete the adjective and adverb chart below. The blank lines at the end are for you to insert your own suggestions.

Adjective	Adverb
rude	
	thoroughly
early	
actual	
	lazily
	well

2. In the table below, pair up each sentence with an adverbial phrase, to create more interesting sentences. Try different pairings and placing the adverbial phrase in different places. Write down your extended sentences.

Sentence	Adverbial phrase
The old man grabbed the money.	after dinner
Mrs Lee made scrumptious cake.	with a wicked grin
A small mouse scuttled away.	in the street
The parrot flew away.	as quickly as possible
They decided to check the cellar again.	for her children

Drama

Think of a scene from a book you have read. Rewrite the extract as a scene from a play, TV show, or film. Continue the scene in any way you wish. Remember to set out your script correctly, with:

- the name of the character speaking in the margin
- stage or film directions in brackets, written in the present tense.

Exciting escapades

Relative pronouns

1. Complete the following sentences by adding the correct relative pronouns.

    a The woman .... lives next-door looks quite scary.

    b I love the cake .... you made today.

    c Danni, ... is a swimming champion, is scared of fish!

    d Farrah, ... son is travelling the world, is a teacher at our school.

    e The huge beast .... was towering over us was a rhinoceros.

    f A police officer, ... car was parked nearby, spotted the thief.

2. Write three sentences using different relative pronouns. In each case, identify the relative pronoun by circling or underlining it.

> **Remember**
>
> Examples of relative pronouns: who, whom, whose, that, which, when, where.

Show and tell

Explain what techniques the writer uses in each of these extracts to create an impression of character.

Extract 1: from *Thief* by Malorie Blackman

1   He was a tall man, as thin as a noodle and with a face that was so sallow it was just about the same colour. His grey-white hair – what there was of it – waved and wandered all over the sides of his head. Flecks of black here and there in his hair made it look as if black
5   pepper had been sprinkled liberally onto a mound of salt.

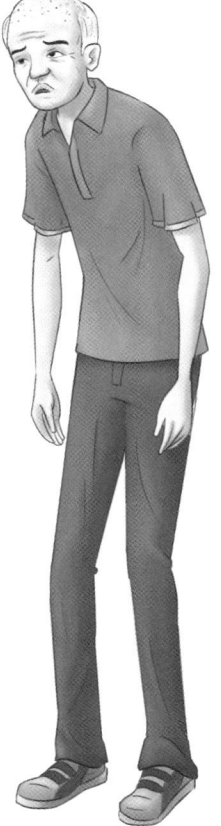

....
....
....
....
....
....

Extract 2: from *Street Child* by Berlie Doherty

1   Jim Jarvis. Want to know who that is? It's me! That's my name. Only thing I've got, is my name. And I've give it away to this man. Barnie, his name is, or something like that. He told me once, only I forgot it, see, and I don't like to ask him again. 'Mister', I call him, to his
5   face, that is. But there's a little space in my head where his name is Barnie. He keeps asking me things. He wants to know my story, that's what he tells me. My story, mister? What d'you want to know that for? Ain't much of a story, mine ain't.

....
....
....
....
....

Exciting escapades

Very short stories

People may not realise it, but tweets are simply stories with a 140-character limit. For example:

> Mum was baking cinnamon cookies in the kitchen. She knows I hate cinnamon. When she turned round, I noticed her eyes were the wrong colour ...

Some stories are even shorter, and can be expressed in six words:

> My stomach hurts. It is lunchtime.

These types of very short stories are sometimes called flash fiction.

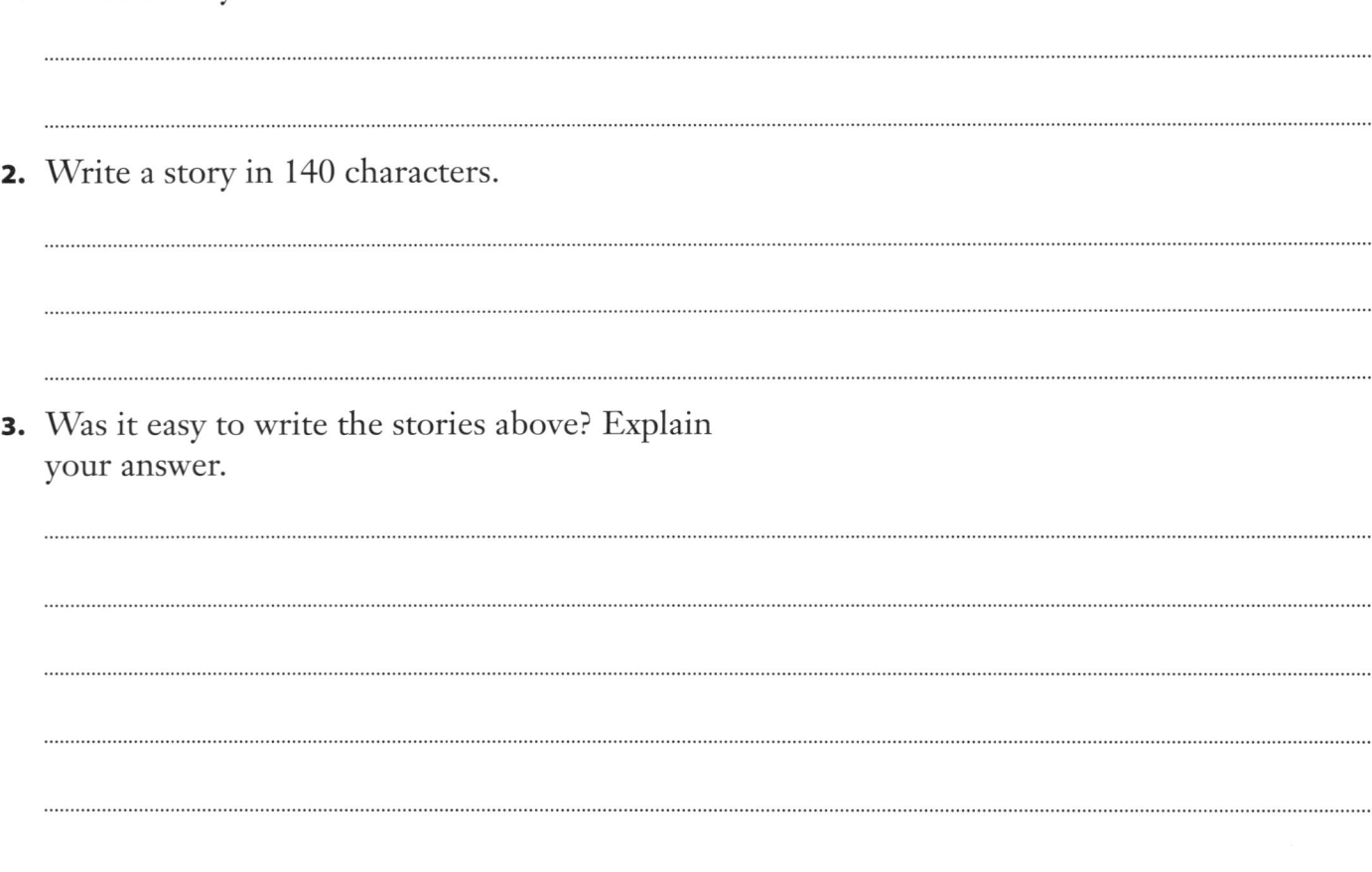

1. Write a story in six words.

   ....

   ....

2. Write a story in 140 characters.

   ....

   ....

   ....

3. Was it easy to write the stories above? Explain your answer.

   ....

   ....

   ....

   ....

   ....

   ....

Exciting escapades quiz

1. Name two techniques that writers use in the openings of books or stories to engage the reader.

   ....

   ....

2. State one way in which you can turn an adjective into an adverb.

   ....

3. Give two examples of adverbs.

   ....

4. Name three techniques that writers use to convey character.

   ....

   ....

5. List some of the vocabulary used to discuss books and stories.

   ....

   ....

   ....

6. When do you use 'who', 'which', or 'that' in relative clauses? Use examples to support your answer.

   ....

   ....

   ....

   ....

7. What is 'flash fiction'?

   ....

   ....

Tremendous television

Soap-box oratory

People who wanted to make speeches in public used to stand on tough crates used for transporting soap. Audiences would assemble round them and join in.

Here's your opportunity to have a say about whatever you feel strongly about.

Start with some practice. Stand on your box in a marketplace and persuade passers-by to buy something. Make your fruit juicy and cheap, or make your kitchen utensil solve all the housewives' problems! You'll need a loud voice.

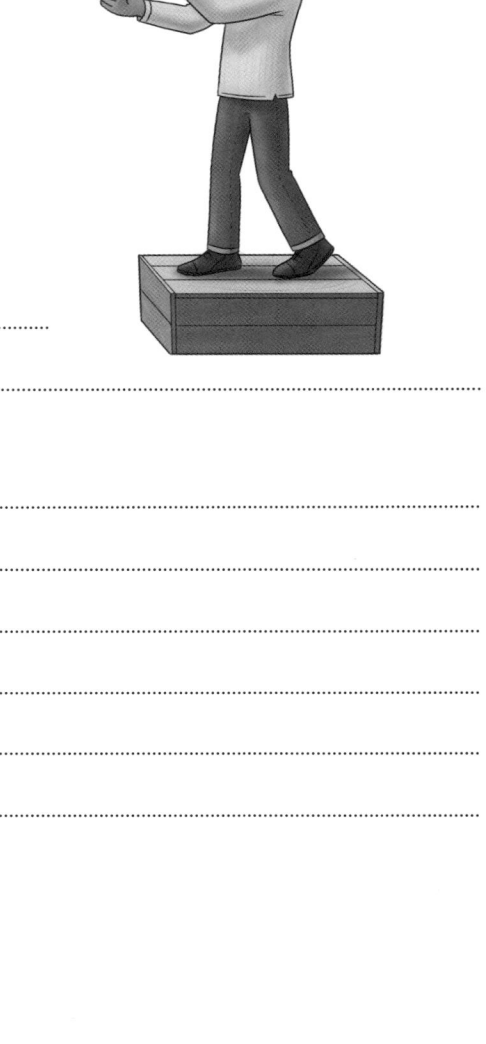

Item for sale is: ....

....

Three ways of persuading passers-by to buy it:

1. ....

....

2. ....

....

3. ....

....

Now choose a pet subject – something you think ought to be done or ought not to be done; something you dislike and think ought to be banned; something that probably few people will agree about.

My pet subject is ....

Three reasons why my audience should agree with me and do something about it:

1. ....

....

2. ....

....

3. ....

....

More interesting prefixes: trans–, cata–, tele–, contra–, hos–, voc–

1. How many words can you think of that begin with 'trans–', meaning 'across?

   ....

   ....

2. 'Cata' means 'down' in Greek. Find four words in your dictionary that seem to fit this meaning.

   i .... **iii** ....

   ii .... **iv** ....

3. 'Tele' means far off. Write sentences to show you know the meanings of these words.

   i Telescope: ....

   ....

   ii Telecommunications: ....

   ....

   iii Telepathy: ....

   ....

4. In the plant opposite, you will find a mixture of words with 'contra–' (against), 'hos–' (a place where guests are received) and 'voc–' (to call or summon). Look up the precise meaning of each word in a dictionary and write them out below.

   ....

   ....

   ....

   ....

   ....

   ....

   ....

   hostel, hotel, vocalist, hospice, hospital, vocation, contradict, contraflow, vociferous, contraband

Tremendous television

The long and the short of it

A little competition: can you write a short short story in 75 words? One extra thing – you must include at least one short sentence for effect. It can be an ordinary sentence or an exclamation or rhetorical question.

Simple.

Here's an example:

> Giorgio woke with a start. He crept to the window just as an enormous gust of wind blew the curtain in his face, and what he saw filled him with fear. Emerging from the trees was a monster with terrible jaws, growling as it approached the house. What was it? Giorgio stood rooted to the spot as the monster came nearer, raising its paw, threatening, roaring, a nightmare. Giorgio woke with a start.

Now write your story below. When you have finished, share your story with other students and see who has made the best, complete one.

I don't agree with you

Here's another chance for you to give your own opinions.

In her letter to *Mothers and Children*, Ms Ryan said she was worried about the effect that TV had on young people. She wanted them to spend less time 'gawking' at TV and be outside more. She didn't like teenage comedy shows and thought there were too many police dramas. She had a special dislike of commercials. Overall, she didn't think that TV was suitable for young people.

Answer her letter. Remember to give a brief introduction and say what you think of her ideas. Don't be rude – make your points clearly and sensibly. Think of a good line to finish with.

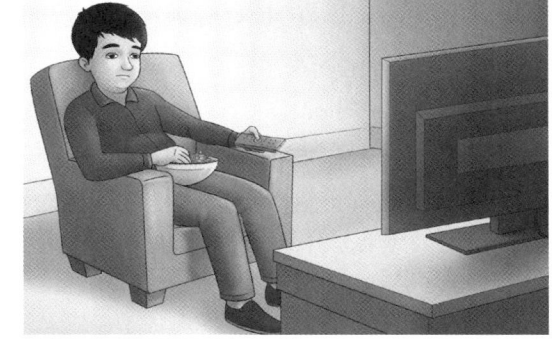

Dear Ms Ryan,

....

....

....

....

....

....

....

....

....

....

....

....

....

....

....

Yours sincerely,

Tremendous television

Who, which, and whose

1. Look at this paragraph. It has too many short sentences.

This is Mr Alioke. He is my uncle. He is a very rich man and he owns the Alioke estate. It is a major pineapple-producing complex. He is also a very wise man. His opinion is one I greatly respect.

Rewrite this paragraph in three sentences. Use each of 'who', 'which', and 'whose' once.

....

....

....

....

....

2. Complete these sentences, using 'who', 'which', and 'whose'.

I threw the ball to my sister ....

....

Because I had not done my homework I was afraid to face up to my teacher ....

....

I just missed the bus ....

I picked up the kitten whose ....

....

.... whose brothers and sisters had arranged a surprise party that afternoon.

3. Make up your own sentences using:

Who: ....

....

Which: ....

....

Whose: ....

....

All about my school

Discuss how you would make a 15-minute TV documentary about your school.

Make a list of things you would want to include.

1. ....
....
2. ....
3. ....
4. ....
5. ....

Who would you interview?

1. ....
2. ....
3. ....

How would you begin? Write the first few lines of your introduction.

....
....
....
....
....
....
....

Discuss what camera shots you would want to use for the different sections.

Role play the interviews and coverage of the different aspects of school life you will cover, such as:

- a sports team
- school uniform
- the dining hall.

Tremendous television

Checking your work

If you wrote an article for a school publication, the editors would not expect to have to correct the mistakes for you, so you would need to check your work carefully before you hand it in.

Read this opening paragraph for an article on insects and write the correct version below, without any mistakes. Unfortunately, this person was very careless with spelling, punctuation, and grammar.

What would world be like without insects, surpose they were to dissapear tommorow. Well for one thing it would be very quite their would be no buzzing. For another thing we would lose a lot of beauty. We are used to seeing the marvelous colours of butterflys moths dragonflies and beetles. Most serious of all would be the affect on the balance of nature. there would be no bees to collect pollen and honey make for us, their would be no aphids for small birds to eaten. Nearly every insect has a place in our world, we cannot afford to interfere with this delicate balance, we must no destroy habitats and kill creatures with insecticides.

Corrected version

....
....
....
....
....
....
....
....
....
....
....
....
....

Tremendous television quiz

1. Why is speaking in public sometimes called 'soap-box oratory', and what opportunities does it give a speaker?

2. a If 'scopein' means to look at in ancient Greek, what does 'telescope' mean?

   b What have 'catastrophe' and 'downfall' in common?

   c What have a hotel and a hospital in common?

3. The speaker on the soap-box said, 'We're all getting wet, I know. But who cares? We're here for a very important reason.' Why was his question rhetorical?

4. What would you say in response to these students if you were a teacher?

   a 'I write everything in very long sentences because I want to sound clever.'

   b 'I write everything in very short sentences to make them easy to read.'

5. When you responded to Ms Ryan's letter, what did you have to remember about your language, and why is this important?

6. 'This is the man .... guinea fowl flew into my garden.'

   Fill in the gap and say exactly what part of speech you have used.

7. When you check your work, what sort of mistakes are you looking for?

8. Explain the confusion between 'quite' and 'quiet', and 'their' and 'there'.

Language and literacy reference

Active voice versus passive voice – Verbs are active when the subject of the sentence (the agent) does the action. Example: The shark swallowed the fish. Active verbs are used more in informal speech or writing.

Verbs are passive when the subject of the sentence has the action done to it. Example: The fish was swallowed by the shark. Passive verbs are used in more formal writing such as reports. Examples: An eye-witness was interviewed by the police. Results have been analysed by the sales team.

Sometimes turning an active sentence to passive, or vice versa, simply means moving the agent:

- The shark (agent and subject) + verb = active
- The fish (object) + verb = passive

Adjective – An adjective describes a noun or adds to its meaning. They are usually found in front of a noun. Example: Green emeralds and glittering diamonds. Adjectives can also come after a verb. Examples: It was big. They looked hungry. Sometimes you can use two adjectives together. Example: tall and handsome. This is called an adjectival phrase.

Adjectives can be used to describe degrees of intensity. To make a comparative adjective you usually add –er (or use more). Examples: quicker; more beautiful. To make a superlative you add –est (or use most). Examples: quickest; most beautiful.

Adverb – An adverb adds further meaning to a verb. Many are formed by adding -ly to an adjective. Example: slow/slowly. They often come next to the verb in a sentence. Adverbs can tell the reader: how – quickly, stupidly, amazingly; where – there, here, everywhere; when – yesterday, today, now; how often – occasionally, often.

Adverbial phrase – The part of a sentence that tells the reader when, where or how something happens is called an adverbial phrase. It is a group of words that functions as an adverb. Example: I'm going to the dentist **tomorrow morning** (when); The teacher spoke to us **as if he was in a bad mood** (how); Sam ran **all the way home** (where). These adverbials are called adverbials of time, manner and place.

Alliteration – Alliteration occurs when two or more nearby words start with the same sound. Example: A slow, sad, sorrowful song.

Antecedent – An antecedent is the person or thing to which the pronoun refers back. Example: President Alkira realised that his life was in danger. 'President Alkira' is the antecedent here.

Antonym – An antonym is a word or phrase that means the opposite of another word or phrase in the same language. Example: shut is an antonym of open. Synonyms and antonyms can be used to add variation and depth to your writing.

Audience – The readers of a text and/or the people for whom the author is writing; the term can also apply to those who watch a film or to television viewers.

Clause – A clause is a group of words that contains a subject and a verb. Example: I ran. In this clause, I is the subject and ran is the verb.

Cliché – An expression, idiom or phrase that has been repeated so often it has lost its significance.

Colloquial language – Informal, everyday speech as used in conversation; it may include slang expressions. Not appropriate in written reports, essays or exams.

Colon – A colon is a punctuation mark (:) used to indicate an example, explanation or list is being used by the writer within the sentence. Examples: You will need: a notebook, a pencil, a notepad and a ruler. I am quick at running: as fast as a cheetah.

Conjugate – To change the tense or subject of a verb.

Conditional tense – This tense is used to talk about something that might happen. Conditionals are sometimes called 'if' clauses. They can be used to talk imaginary situations or possible real-life scenarios. Examples: If it gets any colder the river will freeze. If I had a million pounds I would buy a zoo.

Conjunction – A conjunction is a word used to link clauses within a sentence such as: and, but, so, until, when, as. Example: He had a book in his hand when he stood up.

Connectives – A connective is a word or a phrase that links clauses or sentences. Connectives can be conjunctions. Example: but, when, because. Connectives can also be connecting adverbs. Example: then, therefore, finally.

Continuous tense – This tense is used to tell you that something is continuing to happen. Example: I am watching football.

Discourse markers – Words and phrases such as on the other hand, to sum up, however, and therefore are called discourse markers because they mark stages along an argument. Using them will make your paragraphs clearer and more orderly.

Exclamation – An exclamation shows someone's feelings about something. Example: What a pity!

Exclamation mark – An exclamation mark makes a phrase or a short sentence stand out. You usually use it in phrases like 'How silly I am!' and more freely in dialogue when people are speaking. Don't use it at the end of a long, factual sentence, and don't use it too often.

Idiom – An idiom is a colourful expression which has become fixed in the language. It is a phrase which has a meaning that cannot be worked out from the meanings of the words in it. Examples: 'in hot water' means 'in trouble'; It's raining cats and dogs.

Imagery – A picture in words, often using a metaphor or simile (figurative language) which describes something in detail: writers use visual, aural (auditory) or tactile imagery to convey how something looks, sounds or feels in all forms of writing, not just fiction or poetry. Imagery helps the reader to feel like they are actually there.

Irregular verb – An irregular verb does not follow the standard grammatical rules. Each has to be learned as it does not follow any pattern. For example, catch becomes caught in the past tense, not catched.

Metaphor – A metaphor is a figure of speech in which one thing is actually said to be the other. Example: This man is a lion in battle.

Non-restrictive clause – A non-restrictive clause provides additional information about a noun. They can be taken away from the sentence and it will still make sense. They are separated from the rest of the sentence by commas (or brackets). Example: The principal, who liked order, was shocked and angry.

Onomatopoeia – Words that imitate sounds, sensations or textures. Example: bang, crash, prickly, squishy.

Paragraph – A group of sentences (minimum of two, except in modern fiction) linked by a single idea or subject. Each paragraph should contain a topic sentence. Paragraphs should be planned, linked and organised to lead up to a conclusion in most forms of writing.

Parenthetical phrase – A parenthetical phrase is a phrase that has been added into a sentence which is already complete, to provide additional information. It is usually separated from other clauses using a pair of commas or a pair of brackets (parentheses). Examples: The leading goal scorer at the 2014 World Cup – James Rodriguez, playing for Columbia – scored five goals. The leading actor in the film, Hollywood great Gene Kelly, is captivating.

Passive voice – See active voice.

Person (first, second or third) – The first person is used to talk about oneself – I/we. The second person is used to address the person who is listening or reading – you. The third person is used to refer to someone else – he, she, it, they.

- I feel like I've been here for days. (first person)
- Look what you get, when you join the club. (second person)
- He says it takes real courage. (third person)

Personification – Personification can work at two levels: it can give an animal the characteristics of a human, and it can give an abstract thing the characteristics of a human or an animal. Example: I was looking Death in the face.

Prefix – A prefix is an element placed at the beginning of a word to modify its meaning. Prefixes include: dis-, un-, im-, in-, il-, ir-. Examples: impossible, inconvenient, irresponsible.

Preposition – A preposition is a word that indicates place (on, in), direction (over, beyond) or time (during, on) among others.

Pronoun – A pronoun is a word that can replace a noun, often to avoid repetition. Example: I put the book on the table. It was next to the plant. 'It' refers back to the book in first sentence.

- Subject pronouns act as the subject of the sentence: I, you, he, she, it.
- Object pronouns act as the object of the sentence: me, you, him, her, it, us, you, them.
- Possessive pronouns how that something belongs to someone: mine, yours, his, hers, its, ours, yours, theirs.
- Demonstrative pronouns refer to things: this, that, those, these.

Questions – There are different types of questions.

- Closed questions – This type of question can be answered with a single-word response, can be answered with 'yes' or 'no', can be answered by choosing from a list of possible answers and identifies a piece of specific information.
- Open questions – This type of question cannot be answered with a single-word response, it requires a more thoughtful answer than just 'yes' or 'no'.
- Leading questions – This type of question suggests what answer should be given. Example: Why are robot servants bad for humans? This suggests to the responder that robots are bad as the question is "why are they bad?" rather than "do you think they are bad?" Also called loaded questions.
- Rhetorical question – Rhetorical questions are questions that do not require an answer but serve to give the speaker an excuse to explain his/her views. Rhetorical questions should be avoided in formal writing and essays. Example: Who wouldn't want to go on holiday?

Register – The appropriate style and tone of language chosen for a specific purpose and/or audience. When speaking to your friends and family you use an informal register whereas you use a more formal tone if talking to someone older, in a position of authority or who you do not know very well. Example: I'm going to do up the new place. (informal) I am planning to decorate my new flat. (more formal)

Regular verb – A regular verb follows the rules when conjugated (e.g. by adding –ed in the past tense, such as walk which becomes walked).

Relative clause – Relative clauses are a type of subordinate clause. They describe or explain something that has just been mentioned using who, whose, which, where, whom, that, or when. Example: The girl who was standing next to the counter was carrying a small dog.

Relative pronoun – A relative pronoun does what it says – it takes an idea and relates it to a person or a thing. Be careful to use 'who' for people and 'which' for things. Example: I talked to your teacher, who told me about your unfinished homework. This is my favourite photo, which shows you the beach and the palm trees.

Restrictive clause – Restrictive clauses identify the person or thing that is being referred to and are vital to the meaning of the sentence. They are not separated from the rest of the sentence by a comma. With restrictive clauses, you can often drop the relative pronoun. Example: The letter [that] I wrote yesterday was lost.

Semi-colon – A semi-colon is a punctuation mark (;) that separates two main clauses. It is stronger than a comma but not as strong as a full stop. Each clause could form a sentence by itself. Example: I like cheese; it is delicious.

Sentence – A sentence is a group of words that expresses a complete thought. All sentences begin with a capital letter and end with a full stop, question mark or exclamation mark.

- Simple sentences are made up of one clause. Example: I am hungry.
- Complex sentence – Complex sentences are made up of one main clause and one, or more, subordinate clauses. A subordinate clause cannot stand on its own and relies on the main clause. Example: When I joined the drama club, I did not know that it was going to be so much fun.
- Compound sentence – Compound sentences are made up of two or more main clauses, usually joined by a conjunction. Example: I am hungry and I am thirsty.

Good writers use sentences of different lengths to vary the pace of their writing. Short sentences can make a strong impact while longer sentences can make text flow.

Simile – A simile is a figure of speech in which two things are compared using the linking words 'like' or 'as'. Example: In battle, he was as brave as a lion.

Simple past tense – This tense us used to tell you that something happened in the past. Only one verb is required. Example: I wore.

Simple present tense – This tense is used to tell you that something is happening now. Only one verb is required. Example: I wear.

Standard English – Standard English is the form of English used in most writing and by educated speakers. It can be spoken with any accent. There are many slight differences between Standard English and local ways of speaking. Example: 'We were robbed' is Standard English but in speech some people say, 'We was robbed.'

Suffix – A suffix is an element placed at the end of a word to modify its meaning. Suffixes include: -ible, -able, -ful, -less. Example: useful, useless, meaningful, meaningless.

Summary – A summary is a record of the main points of something you have read, seen or heard. Keep to the point and keep it short. Use your own words to make everything clear.

Synonym – A synonym is a word or phrase that means nearly the same as another word or phrase in the same language. Example: shut is a synonym of close. Synonyms and antonyms can be used to add variation and depth to your writing.

Syntax – The study of how words are organised in a sentence.

Tense – A tense is a verb form that shows whether events happen in the past, present or the future.

- The Pyramids are on the west bank of the River Nile. (present tense)
- They were built as enormous tombs. (past tense)
- They will stand for centuries to come. (future tense)

Most verbs change their spelling by adding –ed to form the past tense. Example: walk/walked. Some have irregular spellings. Example: catch/caught.

Topic sentence – The key sentence of a paragraph that contains the principal idea or subject being discussed.

Word cloud dictionary

Word and definition

24/7 *adverb*
Twenty-four hours a day, seven days a week; all the time.

Accept *verb*
To take a thing that is offered or presented to you; to say yes to an invitation or offer.

Account *noun*
A description or story about something that happened.

Ambush *verb*
To lie in wait for someone in order to attack them.

Ancient *adjective*
Belonging to the distant past; very old.

Apocalypse *noun*
The complete final destruction of the world, as described in the biblical book of Revelation.

Are you dissing…?
An expression that means are you speaking disrespectfully or criticising…?

Assess *verb*
To decide or estimate the value or quality of a person or thing.

Atom *noun*
The smallest particle of a chemical element.

Awful *adjective*
Very bad.

Biodiversity *noun*
The variety of plant and animal life in a particular area.

Biotechnology *noun*
The use of living micro-organisms and biological processes in industrial and commercial production.

Blow *verb*
To be moved or carried by air or the wind.

Brittle *adjective*
Hard but easy to break or snap.

Calamity *noun*
An event that causes great damage or distress.

Calcium *noun*
A chemical substance found in teeth, bones, and lime.

Carbohydrate *noun*
A compound of carbon, oxygen, and hydrogen (e.g. sugar or starch) found in food and a source of energy.

Cataclysm *noun*
A violent upheaval or disaster.

Catastrophe *noun*
A sudden great disaster.

Notes

Word cloud dictionary

Word and definition

Cavernous *adjective*
A cavernous room or space is a huge empty one.

Cereal *noun*
A grass producing seeds which are used as food, e.g. wheat, barley, or rice; a breakfast food made from these seeds.

Character *noun*
A person appearing in a story, film, or play.

Classical *adjective*
To do with ancient Greek or Roman literature or art; classical art or music is serious or conventional in style, and is often associated with the 18th century in Europe.

Cliff hanger *noun*
A tense and exciting ending to an episode of a story.

Clump *noun*
A cluster or mass of things or people.

Collide *verb*
To crash into something.

Colossal *adjective*
Extremely large; enormous.

Cool crystal blue *adjective*
Of a colour intermediate between green and violet, as of the sky or sea on a sunny day, as of frozen ice.

Concerned *adjective*
Worried or anxious about something; involved in or affected by something.

Confusedly heaped *adverb/verb*
Lying in a disorganized pile.

Conservation tillage *noun*
A method of farming that leaves the residue of the previous year's crops on fields before and after planting the next crop.

Contestant *noun*
A person taking part in a contest; a competitor.

Creative *adjective*
Showing imagination and thought as well as skill.

Crescent *noun*
A narrow curved shape coming to a point at each end.

Cultivation *noun*
The action of using land to grow crops; the process of growing or developing things by looking after them.

Debacle *noun*
A complete failure or disaster.

Deep *adjective*
Going a long way down or back or in.

Deliver *verb*
To take letters or goods to the person or place they are addressed to.

Notes

Word cloud dictionary

Word and definition	Notes

Deplete *verb*
To reduce the supply of something by using up large amounts.

Destroy *verb*
To damage something so badly that it is completely spoiled.

Diet *noun*
The sort of foods usually eaten by a person or animal; special meals that a person eats in order to be healthy or to reduce weight.

Discontented *adjective*
Noun discontent, lack of contentment; dissatisfaction.

Drapery *noun*
Cloth arranged in loose folds.

Dude *noun*
A person; a man.

Dull thud *noun*
A muffled, heavy sound, such as that made by an object falling to the ground.

Ecology *noun*
The study of living things in relation to each other and to where they live.

Elliptical *adjective*
Shaped like an ellipse.

Enduring *adjective*
Verb to endure, to suffer or put up with difficulty or pain; to continue to exist, to last.

Engage *verb*
To engage someone's interest or attention is to attract and retain their attention.

Extraordinary *adjective*
Very unusual or strange.

Fantasy *noun*
An imaginative piece of music or writing.

Fat *noun*
A white greasy substance found in animal bodies and certain seeds; oil or grease used in cooking.

Fiasco *noun*
A humiliating or embarrassing failure.

Frightening *adjective*
Verb to frighten, to make someone afraid; to become afraid; to be frightened of someone or something is to fear them.

Fringe *noun*
A decorative edging with many threads hanging down loosely.

Gallop *verb*
To go at the pace of a gallop; to run fast; to proceed at great speed.

Gateway *noun*
An opening containing a gate; a frame or arch built over a gate.

Word cloud dictionary

Word and definition

Gawk *verb*
To stare openly and stupidly.

Glance *verb*
To look at something briefly.

Glare *verb*
To stare angrily or fiercely; to shine with a bright or dazzling light.

Glassy *adjective*
Noun glass, a hard brittle substance that is usually transparent or translucent; a container for drinking from, made of glass; a mirror; a lens or optical instrument.

Grind *verb*
To crush something into tiny pieces or powder; to sharpen or smooth something by rubbing it on a rough surface.

Grip *noun*
A firm hold.

Harmony *noun*
A pleasant combination of musical notes.

Haul *verb*
To pull or drag something with great effort.

Hem *verb*
To hem someone in is to surround them and prevent them from leaving.

Herbicide *noun*
A substance for killing plants.

Hesitate *verb*
To be slow or uncertain in doing or saying something.

Hold your horses
An expression that means wait a moment.

Hollow *adjective*
Having an empty space inside, not solid.

Iconic *adjective*
Very famous or popular; widely recognized and well-established.

Imagination *noun*
The ability to imagine things; the ability to be creative or inventive.

Immediacy *noun*
The quality of bringing one into direct and instant involvement with something, giving rise to a sense of urgency or excitement.

Incredible *adjective*
Impossible to believe; extremely good.

Indecision *noun*
The inability to make decisions; hesitation.

Independent *adjective*
Not dependent on any person or thing for help, money, or support; not connected or involved with something.

Infinitesimal *adjective*
Extremely small.

Word cloud dictionary

Word and definition

Inhospitable *adjective*
Unfriendly to visitors; giving no shelter or good weather.

Insecticide *noun*
A substance for killing insects.

Insecure *adjective*
Not secure or safe; lacking confidence about yourself.

Inspiration *noun*
A sudden brilliant idea; a person or thing that fills you with ideas or enthusiasm.

Intimidate *verb*
To frighten someone with threats into doing something.

Intonation *noun*
The tone or pitch of the voice in speaking; intoning.

Kid *noun*
A child.

Layer *noun*
A single thickness or coating.

Legend *noun*
An old story handed down from the past, which may or may not be true.

Limp *verb*
To walk with difficulty because of an injury to your leg or foot.

Malevolent *adjective*
Wishing to harm people.

Multifarious *adjective*
Of many kinds, very varied.

Myth *noun*
An old story containing ideas about ancient times or about supernatural beings.

Nightmare *noun*
A frightening dream; an unpleasant experience.

Not necessarily *phrase*
(As a response) what has been said or suggested may not be true or unavoidable.

Novel *noun*
A story of fiction that fills a whole book.

Nudge *verb*
To poke a person gently with your elbow.

Nutrient *noun*
A nourishing substance.

Nutritious *adjective*
Giving good nourishment.

Oil *verb*
To put oil on something.

Notes

Word cloud dictionary

Word and definition

OK *adverb, adjective*
All right.

Old-fashioned *adjective*
Of the kind that was usual a long time ago, no longer fashionable.

Open *adjective*
Allowing access, passage, or a view through an empty space; not closed or blocked.

Opportunity *noun*
A good chance to do a particular thing.

Oval-shaped *adjective*
Having a rounded and slightly elongated outline or shape like that of an egg.

Overawe *verb*
To overcome or inhibit someone with awe.

Paralyse *verb*
To cause paralysis in a person or a part of the body; to be paralysed with fear or emotion is to be so affected by it that you cannot act.

Participate *verb*
To take part in something or have a share in it.

Perfect *verb*
To make a thing completely free from faults or defects; make as good as possible.

Perfection *noun*
A perfect state or achievement.

Perpetual *adjective*
Lasting for a long time, occurring repeatedly, continual.

Pesticide *noun*
A substance for killing harmful insects and other pests.

Pitch *noun*
The highness or lowness of a voice or a musical note.

Pitted *adjective*
Having a hollow or indentation on the surface.

Poison *noun*
A substance that can harm or kill a living thing if swallowed or absorbed into the body.

Pound *verb*
To run or go heavily.

Preen *verb*
A bird preens its feathers when it smooths them with its beak.

Prestigious *adjective*
Inspiring respect and admiration; having high status.

Primitive *adjective*
At an early stage of civilization; at an early stage of development, not complicated or sophisticated.

Notes

Word cloud dictionary

Word and definition

Prod *verb*
To poke something or someone; to stimulate someone into action.

Protein *noun*
A substance that is found in all living things and is an essential part of the food of animals.

Race *noun*
A competition to be the first to reach a particular place or to do something.

Rap sheet *noun*
A report, school file; a criminal record.

Redundant *adjective*
No longer needed or useful; superfluous.

Renowned *adjective*
Famous or celebrated.

Repertoire *noun*
A stock of songs, plays, jokes etc. that a person or company knows and can perform.

Rhythm *noun*
The regular pattern of beats or stresses in a piece of speech or music; a regularly recurring sequence of movements or events; adverb rhythmically.

Rough-work *verb*
To create a first draft of something.

Run *verb*
To move with quick steps so that both or all feet leave the ground at each stride.

Rush *verb*
To go or move quickly.

Satisfy *italic*
To give someone what they need or want.

Scant *adjective*
Barely enough or adequate.

Scatter *verb*
To throw or send things in all directions; to run or leave quickly in all directions.

Senility *noun*
The condition of being senile: weak or confused and forgetful because of old age.

Sever *verb*
To cut or break something off.

Shadow *noun*
The dark shape that falls on a surface when something is between the surface and a light; an area of shade.

Word cloud dictionary

Word and definition

Shrink *verb*
To become smaller, or to make something smaller.

Signify *verb*
To mean something.

Sitch *noun*
Situation

Slack *adjective*
Not pulled or held tight, loose; not busy, not working hard.

Sleep *noun*
The condition or time of rest in which the eyes are closed, the body relaxed, and the mind unconscious.

Snow-slip *noun*
A mass of snow falling rapidly downhill.

Squirm *verb*
To wriggle about when you feel embarrassed or awkward.

Stagger *verb*
To walk unsteadily.

Still *adjective*
Not moving; not disturbed by wind or sounds.

Stout *adjective*
Thick and strong.

Strand *noun*
Each of the threads or wires twisted together to form a rope, yarn or cable.

Strap *verb*
To fasten or bind something with a strap or straps.

Strike *verb*
To hit someone or something.

Stuff *noun*
Miscellaneous things.

Sunken *adjective*
Sunk deeply into a surface.

Sustainability *noun*
Verb to sustain, to keep someone alive; to keep something happening; to undergo or suffer something harmful or unpleasant; to support or uphold something.

The price of fame *noun*
The result of being well-known.

Threat *noun*
A warning that you will punish, hurt, or harm a person or thing; a sign of something undesirable; a person or thing causing danger.

Throw *verb*
To put something in a place carelessly or hastily.

Time-honoured *adjective*
Respected or valued because it has existed for a long time.

Word cloud dictionary

Word and definition

Torrent *noun*
A rushing stream, a great flow; a heavy downpour of rain.

Totally awesome man
An expression that means really impressive you know.

Tradition *noun*
A belief or custom passed down from one generation to another.

Traumatise *verb*
To shock or distress someone in a way that produces a lasting effect on their mind.

Trudge *verb*
To walk slowly and wearily.

Unearthly *adjective*
Unnaturally strange and frightening; very awkward or inconvenient.

Unique *adjective*
Being the only one of its kind; unlike any other.

Unprecedented *adjective*
That has never happened or been done before.

Unrequited *adjective*
Unrequited love is not returned or rewarded.

Variety *noun*
A quantity of different kinds of things.

Veer *verb*
To change direction, to swerve.

Vicious *adjective*
Cruel and aggressive; severe or violent.

Vitamin *noun*
Any of a number of substances that are present in various foods and are essential to keep people and animals healthy.

Volume *noun*
The strength or power of sound produced by a radio, television, or other equipment.

Wall *noun*
Something that serves as a block or barrier.

Wither *verb*
To become dried up and shrivelled; to fade away or fall into decline.

Worse *adjective*
More bad; less good.

Wrench *verb*
To twist or pull something violently.

Yell *verb*
To give a loud cry, to shout.

Yield *verb*
To produce as a natural product or profit.

Notes